BELIEVE

SALLY PEARSON

BELIEVE

AN INSPIRATIONAL STORY OF AIMING HIGH

SALLY PEARSON WITH SCOTT GULLAN

hardie grant books

MELBOURNE · LONDON

To you, the reader.
Believing in yourself is only the beginning.
Enjoy the ride and never give up.

Published in 2013 by Hardie Grant Books

Hardie Grant Books (Australia)
Ground Floor, Building 1
658 Church Street
Richmond, Victoria 3121
www.hardiegrant.com.au

Hardie Grant Books (UK)
Dudley House, North Suite
34–35 Southampton Street
London WC2E 7HF
www.hardiegrant.co.uk

Cataloguing in publications data available from the National Library of Australia
Believe by Sally Pearson
ISBN 9781742706368

Cover design by Luke Causby / BlueCork
Cover images courtesy of Getty Images
Typesetting by Kirby Jones
Typeset in ITC Esprit Std 12/18.5pt
Colour reproduction by Splitting Image Colour Studio
Printed and bound in Australia by Griffin Press

Acknowledgements

To my mum, Anne, who didn't see my hyperactive personality as a cause for concern but as a sign of my potential as an elite athlete: thank you for always believing in me and for introducing me to the world of sport. You were always there cheering me on at my sporting carnivals, and you are and always will be my number one fan. I love you.

To my coaches, Sharon and Peter Hannan, for your passion and love for the sport; I have never seen anything like it from any other coach in the world. The persistence and patience you have shown throughout my career is second to none and I can't thank you enough or be any more grateful for what you've done. And thank you, Sharon, for sticking by me through all the emotional rollercoasters we've had.

To my manager, Robert Joske, who saw a talent in me and took me on at a young age so that I could turn athletics into a living and make life easier for my mum, who worked two jobs to help me realise my Olympic dream.

To my whole support crew, who have stuck by me for the last fourteen years: physiotherapist Britt Caling, massage therapist Thea Dillon, psychologist Andrea Furst, racing agents Maurie Plant and Brian Roe, physiotherapist Bruce Rawson, sports physician Dr Paul Ohmsen, specialist musculoskeletal physiotherapist Dr Kerrie Evans and podiatrist Ashley Mahoney. There are many people who are a part of the Pearson camp, and I trust you all to keep me at my best both physically and mentally. You have never failed me and I appreciate everything you have done.

To Scott Gullan: without him, this book would not be possible. Thanks for helping me put everything into perspective and realise that life is about having fun and staying relaxed.

To General Peter Cosgrove: a big thank you for generously providing the foreword and for launching my first book. I have admired you from the day we first met and I have valued your feedback, friendship and mentorship ever since.

I would also like to thank Hardie Grant Books, especially publisher Pam Brewster, editor Allison Hiew and publicist Monica Svarc. You have worked so hard to make this book a reality; thank you simply isn't enough.

To my sponsors, who have made my athletics career that much easier. I remember when I signed my first Adidas contract; my life changed for the better, forever. Impossible really is nothing! To AMP, who saw an up-and-coming talent in me that they wanted to help and support.

I am grateful and appreciate everything that you have done for me. To everyone who has supported me over the years: Athletics Australia, Queensland Academy of Sport, John Brown and everyone at the Sport and Tourism Youth Foundation, Athletics International, Mitsubishi, Acer, Qantas, Coles and Omega. Without your help, my focus and attention to detail would not be the same.

Last but by no means least, to my three favourite boys in the whole world: Kieran, Oscar and Toby. You don't understand what you do for me just by being there. To my fur babies, Oscar and Toby, I know you won't be able to read this but I still want to note that you two, no matter how my day has been, are always waiting to greet me as I walk through the door. You make me smile; you make me frustrated; you make me crazy at times, but you will

always have a smile on your faces and that's all I can ever ask for.

Kieran, my husband, you didn't ask for a life on the road with an elite athlete; you didn't ask for the rollercoaster life and for sometimes bearing the brunt of bad training sessions or bad races, but you have stayed for some reason. I thank you and I love you for understanding that most of the time I need to be selfish and look after myself before anyone else. Thank you for taking this ride and dropping everything to be by my side. I love you.

Contents

Foreword

Over the past seven decades, this nation has given rise to some of the most marvellous track and field athletes to compete on the international stage: 'Golden Girls' Betty Cuthbert and Shirley Strickland de la Hunty, Herb Elliott, John Landy, Ron Clarke, Robert 'Deeks' de Castella, Steve 'Mona' Moneghetti – and so many others. More recently, we rejoiced in the triumph of Cathy Freeman who, as she carried a nation around the Sydney Olympic track to a timeless victory in *that* race, seemed to us all to be there and yet somehow not. How did she do it; how did she feel? We never really knew, because it is possible that even Cathy herself was not sure.

And then there is Sally Pearson, truly a national athletic treasure, surely the Australian athlete we would all hope to be like: flesh and blood, but possessed of an iron will and diamond focus – a winner if ever there was one. If Cathy somehow found the speed and strength to win, then there is no doubt about how Sally came to be the best hurdler in the world: she works and works and works; she never stops and never gives up and refuses to accept that any competitor will beat her on the day. No doubt dilettante sports scientists would tell you that she is either too short (or too tall) and perhaps that ideally from hip to knee to foot she should be several centimeters longer. But this matters not to her, certainly not to us and most definitely not to her opponents, who see only her steely gaze at race time and her blinding speed as she pulls away from them.

It is absorbing to read an account at the end of an elite athlete's career, but so much more gripping to read about them when the competitive fire burns brighter than ever and they are at the pinnacle of their event. How did they get there and how do they keep on doing it?

Believe is not only a story about racing, but also about life and relationships: Sally's redoubtable Mum, her marvellous coach Sharon and Sally's rock, her husband Kieran.

We're a sporting nation; we can't help ourselves, we love winners. *Believe* is a story about winning by never giving in, about a ceaseless quest by one of our champions, about our Sally. It's a great and ongoing story.

General Peter Cosgrove, AC, MC (Retired)

Introduction

I'm winning the Olympics.

I was over the sixth hurdle and my mind was already focused ahead to number eight because in both the heat and the semifinal I'd hit it.

That was a mistake. Instead of attacking it hard, I reached for it and went too high, clearing it by too much and slowing my momentum. I was playing safe.

Don't worry. Keep going; you're still winning.

I cleared the final hurdle, feeling that customary wave of relief: I was safe and all that was left was running over the finish. That's the fun part. I was particularly enjoying the moment because I still couldn't sense anyone around me.

Yeeeessss … Oh no, hang on.

As soon as I crossed the line I looked over at the clock and saw the time – 12.35 seconds. Then I turned and she was there. Dawn Harper was right there.

*Oh God no. Surely not. I can't have just lost my
Olympic gold medal.*

I hadn't seen her until we were probably 2 metres past the finish line. She was close – too close. But I was sure I was ahead of her when it mattered, although there were still no names up on the big screen.

*Why is it taking so long? I know I've won. I know I've
won. I know I've won. I know I've won.*

After all I'd been through, over the previous two weeks in particular, all I could do was believe. I had to believe. Then the names appeared.

Oh my God, I'm the Olympic champion.

We were a
competitive bunch,
and even at the
age of ten I hated
to lose.

1

'Can you please let me win?'

I looked over at the girl who was politely asking the question. We were about to race each other in the school sports at my latest primary school in Sydney. I was the new kid on the block and I'd been told she was the best runner in Year 3 at La Perouse Public School.

'Oh yeah, sure,' I said with a smile.

And I was genuine … until the gun went off. Then I became a different person.

There was no way in the world I was going to let her win the race. Something had kicked in and I ran as fast as I could to the finish line. I won the race and received a very confused look from my rival. Already my hatred of losing was inbuilt.

It got me some new friends, though, as everyone kept coming up to me, saying, 'You can run pretty fast, can't you?'

'Yeah,' would be my embarrassed reply.

My PE teacher apparently saw it too because he wrote in my report card: 'Sally has the ability to become an elite athlete one day.'

I was pretty excited to read that, as that was a goal of mine, but it wasn't going to be as a runner; I was going to be a gymnast. It had been my one passion from very early in life.

My mother, Anne, loves telling the story about how at the age of one – I was walking by eight and a half months – she took me down to the park with some neighbouring children.

They were older than me and were playing on the monkey bars. She says I somehow managed to pull myself up onto the bars and immediately hung upside down.

'Well, you're going into gymnastics, then,' was her immediate thought.

I started when I was four years old. I would do a gymnastics class and then walk across the park and do swimming lessons. That lasted for about a year before the timetables were changed and I was forced to pick one over the other. I went with gymnastics and was quickly put into the elite squad.

Bouncing and jumping all over the place suited my personality because, as my mother kept telling me, I was crazy. I would often stand at the top of the stairs in our home and, as soon as Mum walked past, I'd leap out at her and expect her to catch me. I had so much energy, and I think that's a big reason why she steered me towards sport.

Gymnastics quickly became serious, and by the age of seven I was training up to 30 hours a week. Twice a week I would train at 6 am and Mum would drop me off, as it was on her bus route into the city, where she worked.

The gymnastics coach would then take me to school, which at that stage was Coogee Public School, but we'd usually be around 15–20 minutes late. I would have to go to the office and get a late slip to take to the teachers to explain why I was late. I just wrote, 'At gymnastics.' This worked for a couple of days before the questions started.

'Is this going to be happening all the time?'

'I only do it twice a week in the mornings,' I responded.

'Okay, then,' was the teacher's response.

A couple of weeks later a letter was sent home from the principal, saying I had to choose between gymnastics and school because they weren't going to allow me to be late anymore.

It was a no-brainer, and Mum agreed. I changed schools.

Gymnastics was pretty full on, as the trainers pushed us hard at that young age because we weren't scared of anything. The theory was that the older we got, the greater the chance that the fear factor, with regards to the height of the bars and beam, would set in.

My best apparatus was the vault, because of my speed, and I was quite good at doing the giant rings on the bars. The beam was by far my worst; I was hopeless and couldn't stand it because I didn't have the patience for it. The floor routine was always interesting, because I could never remember the whole routine and was constantly getting into trouble for forgetting what to do next.

I competed at the NSW state championships, but most of the time we would take part in team events representing our club, Bunnerong. There had been a group of us who'd started together and gone through the ranks in the elite squad. We were a competitive bunch, and even at the age of ten I hated to lose.

At one particular competition I remember, Bunnerong had three teams of three athletes each. I was so annoyed with the team I was in, because I thought they weren't good enough. One of the girls hurt her ankle three days before the competition, which added to my frustration, considering I didn't really think the other girl was strong enough.

I may have been a little bit off the mark with that one. Her name was Hayley Tyrell, and she actually ended up being one of the best gymnasts in Australia. But she was clearly a late developer, because it wasn't really happening for us at this competition!

At the end of it we all had to sit down on the floor for the presentation. I had my fingers crossed that we'd won a medal, and when they announced that third place was going to Bunnerong, I got up and was so excited.

It was the wrong team.

I sulked for the rest of the night and, to make matters worse, my lift home was with the girls who'd come third. The whole trip they just sat there beaming, playing with their medals. I was the biggest sore loser.

I loved gymnastics, but a change of scenery was to alter the course of my life forever.

* * *

My mum was born in England, one of five girls, and came to Australia on a holiday with her cousin in 1981. She ended up staying.

On 19 September 1986 I came into the world, and it's just been us ever since, given my father has never been on the scene.

From when I was five months old, Mum used to work long hours – and sometimes even two jobs – to make ends meet. In 1995 we moved from Sydney to the Gold Coast in search of a better life.

One of our first tasks was to find a gymnastics club. We joined the Southport Gymnastics Club and I immediately didn't like it. It was a very cliquey environment, and I felt like an outcast and wasn't really made welcome. I was also a very shy and sensitive kid who hated feeling like people were making fun of me.

'I don't want to do this anymore,' I told Mum after just my third training session. She tried to change my mind, given she knew how much I loved the sport, but I hated the way I'd been treated.

By chance, a new Little Athletics club was just opening up at Helensvale around the same time, and Mum had me there on day one. I'd always enjoyed running at school, so she suggested we give it a go. It would prove to be an inspired decision. I quickly identified my four favourite events: the 100m, 200m, high jump and long jump.

The problem was, there weren't many girls at my club, so it wasn't long before I was competing against the boys. Given how shy I was, I didn't want to be around the boys or have to talk to them all the time. In the end, that was the reason I moved to Ashmore Little Athletics, where there was a big group of girls and I instantly felt a lot more comfortable.

I had started to win my fair share of medals and, by 1999, when I was in my last year of primary school, I was taking part in state and national championships.

It was at the Little Athletics state championships in March of that year in Townsville that I met the woman who would change my life. Her name was Sharon Hannan.

Unbeknown to me, my mother had been introduced to Sharon, who coached a squad on the Gold Coast close to where we lived, just before I raced in the final of the 200m hurdles. They watched me win the race, and Sharon turned to Mum and said, 'She's fast.'

Mum asked if she would coach me, but Sharon pointed out that with the national championships just three weeks away there was no point starting then. She told her to send me down in May, after the season break. Normally Sharon didn't coach primary school kids, but because I was almost 13 – a year older than most in Grade 7 – she was prepared to bend the rules.

I was so nervous going down to the track for my first session with her.

'Wow, you've grown, haven't you?' Sharon said.

'I don't know, have I?' I thought, 'Who's this strange lady?' I didn't even know her and she was saying I'd grown.

It felt like the first day at a new school. I didn't know anyone in the training group, and for the first few weeks it was tough, but I was very good at doing what I was told. I just went with the flow. I didn't question Mum about why I needed a coach; I just did what she wanted. And whatever Sharon told me to do, I did without question.

The reason I was getting serious about running wasn't because I wanted to do it. It was more because everyone else was doing it, and I just wanted to be with the in crowd.

It's funny when I hear other people's stories about how they knew from day one that they wanted to be an Olympic champion. I never thought like that when I was young. I knew I was competitive when I was in a race, but outside of that I was just along for the ride.

Then along came the Sydney Olympics.

'How do I do that?' I wondered. 'How do you train to be the best athlete in the world?'

2

I t was the only race I watched.

Kneeling down on the floor, I got as close as I could to the TV screen to see her. Cathy Freeman looked amazing in her hooded jumpsuit and, like millions of others, I was screaming as she hit the front in the home straight to win the Olympic 400m gold medal. I was fascinated by her and what she'd just done.

'How do I do that?' I wondered. 'How do you train to be the best athlete in the world?'

I'd been lucky enough to meet Cathy a couple of years earlier at the opening of the Couran Cove Resort on South Stradbroke Island. A couple of kids from each primary school in the Gold Coast area were selected to meet Cathy and also take part in a clinic with the Great Britain team, which was training at the nearby Runaway Bay complex.

They had us doing a 60m sprint and then some hurdling. I went flat out in the first race, and one of the athletes, whose name was Katherine Merry – she ended up winning the bronze medal behind Cathy in Sydney – approached me afterwards. She seemed surprised at how quick I was, which was pretty cool – although it was a reaction I was starting to get used to receiving from adults.

Our hurdles mentor was former Olympic 100m champion Linford Christie. He was this massive man with dreadlocks, and I was determined to do it exactly the way he showed us. All the other kids managed only one bound over the hurdle, but I kept going. Linford seemed impressed, and I was pumped. I never used to say much, but secretly I liked to use my actions to show off, so I was pretty proud of my efforts.

The day got even better when we finally met Cathy and I got her to sign my cap. She was very quiet and looked like she wanted to be by herself, but everyone was desperate to get a piece of her.

Mum managed to snap a few photos of the two of us, which quickly took pride of place in our house. And now, after the Olympics, it was a picture of me with an Olympic champion!

I couldn't stop thinking about how much her life must have just changed. Mine had certainly gotten a little tougher in 2000, as Sharon introduced hurdles into my life. I thought I was a sprinter, not a hurdler, even though

I dabbled with hurdles in Little Athletics. But my response when my coach suggested it was the same as always: 'Well, I'd better do it then.' The bonus was that I got to train an extra night with the squad, which made me happy. Sharon trained the hurdlers on Monday night and sprinters on Tuesday and Thursday.

I was an expert on the bus routes around the Gold Coast because that was how I got around. We were living in Labrador, so to get to school it took about an hour, given I had to get a bus into Harbour Town, then change to another bus to get out to Helensvale State High School.

Getting to training after school was only one bus ride but, because it stopped so many times to pick up other schoolkids, it took ages. I started training at 5 pm and would wriggle into my running gear on the bus. Normally we'd train for two hours and I'd either get the bus home or get a lift with Sharon or her husband, Peter.

More often than not, my post-training debrief would centre around how much I disliked the hurdles because I hit so many in training and was quickly getting battered and bruised.

My first national high school championships were in Adelaide and I qualified in the 100m, 200m and 90m hurdles. I didn't do very well in the 100m, finishing fifth or sixth, but I was excited to make it to the final of the hurdles, given it was my first season doing them.

The 200m final was first, though, and I was always nervous and sick before doing 200s. It felt like it was just that little bit too far, as I didn't have the speed endurance required just yet. I found something, though, and ran a massive personal best, cracking the 25-second barrier for the first time, finishing third behind two other Queenslanders in 24.92 seconds.

This excitement flowed on to the hurdles final, but something went amiss at the first hurdle and I got on my wrong leg, which completely threw out my rhythm. I tried to pick up pace but overcompensated and ended up smashing into the sixth hurdle and then hitting the deck.

It was so embarrassing, but I had a sneaking suspicion it wasn't the last time the barriers would get the better of me.

* * *

'Why am I here?'

I was so angry at Sharon. We'd just walked into the call room – which was where athletes checked in with officials to confirm their participation before each race – and were only minutes away from walking out on the track for the heats of the Under 20 100m at the 2001 Australian championships in Brisbane.

The under 20! I was only 14.

'What am I doing here?' I kept asking her.

'You are here because you deserve to be,' Sharon said. Her reasoning was that to run my best I had to run against the best, and people who were faster than me.

A month earlier at the under-age national championships in Bendigo I'd won the Under 16 100m and 200m, medalled in the long jump and high jump, and anchored Queensland's 4x100m relay team, which set a new Australian record. The times hadn't been great, though, which is why Sharon was throwing me in the deep end. I didn't like the idea.

'I'm 14 years old,' I kept saying. 'I'm going to be terrible against these girls.'

Thankfully I was wrong, and my coach had gotten it right again. Sharon had wanted some competition, to have faster girls in front of me so I would be pushing to go with them.

The problem with that theory was that they were never in front of me. I not only won my heat but I also smashed the 12-second barrier for the first time, clocking 11.94. The final was even better, and I took out the Australian Under 20 title in 11.91. It was a major breakthrough and Sharon was convinced it was a game-changer.

Suddenly Athletics Australia was keen to talk and we were summoned to a meeting about the World Youth Championships. Both Sharon and I had never heard of such an event.

It turned out that my 11.91-second run had qualified me for the championships, but there was a hitch. AA was saying that because I hadn't set the time in the right age group – I did it in Under 20 and not Under 18 – they weren't going to select me.

'Are you serious?' I said.

We were both bemused. I got the impression they thought my victory was a fluke and that at 14 I wouldn't be able to handle the pressure of racing against older girls on the world stage.

In the end I was like: 'Whatever.'

We weren't too worried about it, and looked at it as just another step on the learning curve that Sharon and I were on together. She'd gotten into the sport almost by accident, and was figuring out on the run what was required to coach at the elite level.

It had all started when her nine-year-old daughter, Richelle, came home from school with a flyer for Little Athletics. They were living in a small town called Gordonvale, south of Cairns, and Sharon was working for a local airline. She started helping out on Sunday mornings at Little A's; her first task was managing the tape measure for the field events.

The next season the people in charge changed it to a Wednesday afternoon, which didn't suit Sharon and another family – the father of that family was a navy captain – so together they decided to start their own club, and Cairns Little Athletics was born.

Funnily enough, after going through all the red tape to set it up, the navy captain was redeployed, so Sharon was left running the whole show. In her first season she had 83 kids sign up.

Realising she'd better get her head around track and field, Sharon went off and did a coaching course. Even when her daughter progressed to junior level, where she became a race walker and got as far as the state championships, she stayed involved as the zone coordinator for Little A's.

And that's how she met her husband, Peter, in 1989. He was an athletics coach from the Gold Coast and was part of a group who'd travelled up there to conduct coaching clinics. They hit it off and started writing to each other. One thing led to another and, when Richelle had finished Year 12 at the end of 1991, they relocated to be with Peter. Sharon and Peter were married on New Year's Eve 1992.

When the Gold Coast City Athletics Track opened in 1998, Sharon, who had been on the track advisory committee, volunteered to be the caretaker for the first few months of its operation. Soon the council realised it was a full-time job and she was appointed caretaker manager until they called for tenders for the management contract. Sharon, and Peter, who had been a part of the Gold Coast Athletics Club for more than 20 years, won the contract, and their company, Sports Credentials, has run the facility ever since.

While Sharon was always reading coaching manuals and asking questions to broaden her knowledge, what she had quickly developed was a penchant for setting big goals. And often she wouldn't even tell me about them before blurting them out at a crucial moment.

One such occasion was during our first meeting with the Australian Olympic Team head coach, Keith Connor. He was a scary man, big in stature, and had an intimidating manner about him.

He had started by asking me about what my goals were in the sport.

'I don't know, I just want to make the Olympics,' I said.

He gave me a look, one almost of disgust.

'What happens when you make the Olympics?' he asked. 'What's going to happen then? Are you just going to stop? You need to have some more specific goals than that.'

I was almost shaking. 'I don't know … I just want to go to the Olympics.'

'That's not enough,' he bellowed. 'Do you want to make the final or get top eight or get a medal?'

'I don't know,' I repeated again. 'I guess I want to win a medal one day.'

Then he paused and it was like something clicked. 'How old are you?'

'I'm only 14.'

Connor looked shocked. 'Oh my God, I'm so sorry. You're a baby.' He was very apologetic, but then Sharon piped up.

'She is going to run 11.6 seconds in the 100m and she's going to make the 2002 Commonwealth Games team in the relay.'

I looked at her with dismay. This was the first I'd heard of such a plan.

'Sharon,' I said, and gave her a dirty look.

She had another crazy plan, which she didn't mention in that meeting, and that was to turn me into a heptathlete. She and Peter had discussed it at length, and they'd introduced me to our best heptathlete of all time: Jane Flemming, the 1990 Commonwealth champion.

They figured I was already a long way down the right track, given my success as a junior in the high jump and long jump. The heptathlon had seven disciplines – 100m hurdles, high jump, shot-put, 200m, long jump, javelin throw and 800m – and it sounded like a whole lot of hard work.

Once again I didn't dismiss it because I was happy to go along with whatever they thought, but for the moment those plans were on hold as I had a sore foot. We'd had it looked at, but the initial diagnosis for my first injury scare was that it was no big deal.

Something told me that was wrong.

In the space of seven days I'd slashed .34 of a second off my personal best. In other words, I'd improved by more than three metres!

3

'You won't be able to do the 200m or the 200m hurdles because you can't run around a bend.'

My heart sank as I listened to the Athletics Australia team doctor, Tim Barbour, explain that my sore foot was actually fractured. It had gone from a hot spot to a stress fracture and was now fully fractured.

We were in Melbourne for the Australian All Schools Championships and I couldn't believe I wasn't going to be doing all my events. As soon as we left the doctor's office, I burst into tears. I think it was a build-up of anger from a tough few months, and it just all overflowed.

Six months earlier we'd had X-rays on the foot that had shown nothing, but I wasn't convinced because it continued to ache. I'd gone to a podiatrist, who showed me how to strap the foot, and he also put some padding in my shoes to try to ease the pain. I ended up having the worst-looking feet, because every time the strapping came off, skin would just peel off with it. Instead of working on the track, Sharon had me exercising in the pool for three months to maintain my fitness base.

I'd managed to compete at the Queensland All Schools and smashed the Australian record in the 200m hurdles, which was why I was so devastated about not being allowed to run it in the nationals. We'd come down to Melbourne a couple of weeks earlier to train with legendary hurdles coach Roy Boyd. Sharon was in awe of his knowledge and wanted him to have a look at our training group to get some advice on technique.

I didn't even get through the first session with Roy because of the foot, and the next day I wasn't even able to break into a jog. Walking seemed to be okay, but as soon as I started to run, it really hurt. That was when we decided I should see the team doctor.

I blamed Sharon for what had happened. Maybe it was just me being an unreasonable teenager, but I didn't want to be around her. I didn't even want to talk to her.

My mood worsened when I was defeated by 1/100th of a second in the 100m by a girl I'd easily defeated at the Queensland state titles. With my anger boiling, I took it out on the field in the 90m hurdles final and smashed the Australian record, running 12.51.

Sitting in the grandstand watching the 200m hurdles was the hardest thing I'd experienced in my short career. It was painful to watch a girl from Tasmania claim the national title in a time that was more than two seconds outside my record.

As soon as I got back to the Gold Coast, they put my foot in a plaster cast. I needed crutches to get around, and for eight weeks that was my life. To make matters worse, it just happened to be one of the hottest summers in recent times in Queensland. I was stuck at home every day and began to question what I was doing. I'd had a horrible year and was constantly asking myself: 'Why am I doing this sport?' To make matters worse, I started to put on weight because I wasn't doing any exercise.

When they eventually let me back into training, there was one major problem: I still couldn't run. In fact, I couldn't even jog because the foot was too sore. And my leg had wasted away to nothing and was as skinny as my forearm.

The option that Sharon came up with was race walking, so while everyone else was zipping around at training, I was waddling along in the outside lane.

It was embarrassing, and the whole period was tough. I felt confused, I felt like I had no friends, and I hated everyone.

The carrot to lure me out of the funk was the world junior championships, which were in Kingston, Jamaica, in 2002.

I was determined to make that team. The problem I had was that the nationals were in April, so were a couple of months' training going to be enough?

They weren't, and I knew that even before I stepped out for the opening round of the Under 20 100m. Twelve months earlier I'd easily beaten the field in my career breakthrough performance. That felt like a lifetime ago.

I finished third in my heat, clocking 12.20 to get through to the final. Apart from my own sorry plight, what was also annoying me was that the girl who was going to win, fellow Queenslander Michelle Cutmore, wasn't going to go to the world juniors. Her coach didn't want her to go, and I was furious that she was even competing if that was the case. It was a big tease. She ended up winning impressively in 11.83 seconds, which further infuriated me when I came sixth.

I didn't make the team.

* * *

High school was an interesting time. I certainly wasn't part of the 'popular' group, except when it came to athletics day.

'You're the runner girl, aren't you?' was the usual question from my fellow Helensvale State High School students.

'My name is Sally, by the way,' was my stock-standard response.

The first few years at high school had been a lot of fun; I had a great circle of friends. But I sensed we started to drift apart the older we became. While I still loved being around them, we were moving in different directions. I was right into athletics and they were off doing other things in their lives. Unfortunately, I started to feel like I couldn't connect with them like I had before. It made me feel lonely, because I wasn't able to talk to them about my running, as they wouldn't understand.

One person at school who I was able to confide in was my PE teacher, Brett Green. He was a big supporter, which helped, given I was always missing heaps of classes because of track commitments. Mr Green had been one of the coaches at my original Little Athletics club, and had told Mum early on that I was 'one of the most balanced athletes' he'd seen. He was always encouraging me to stick with my running.

The problem was that for most of the year just gone, I'd been questioning why I had. Eventually, the wheel slowly started to turn towards the end of 2002. The All Schools nationals were in Tasmania in December, and I managed to get into the final of the 100m. I still wasn't allowed to run bends, which meant the 200m hurdles and the 200m were again off the agenda.

I had no idea how I was going to go, and it was a competitive field led by Michelle Cutmore, the girl who'd won the Under 20 title earlier in the year, and another fast Queenslander, Jacinta Boyd.

For the first time in what seemed like forever, I felt fast throughout the race and managed to claim the win in 11.99

seconds. I was so excited about the time because it was the first time I'd broken 12 seconds for more than a year.

My fitness was clearly improving and my confidence returned instantly. I could feel my love of the sport being rekindled.

The runner girl was back.

* * *

'I just feel like screaming.'

This time I was saying it to Sharon with delight, which was a nice change from the events of the previous couple of years.

We were celebrating my victory in the Under 20 100m at the 2003 national championships in Brisbane. While the win was good, the time was what had me dancing around the warm-up track. I'd just run the fastest time of my career, 11.76, to claim revenge on New Zealand's April Brough.

A day earlier she'd pipped me in the final of the 200m, which, naturally, I didn't take very well. I didn't like a stranger coming into my backyard and beating me, so I was more pumped than usual for the 100m. This time I put a space on her – she ran second in 12.02 seconds – and it turned out my winning time would've got me third place in the open national final.

The victory booked me a spot on my first Australian team for the World Youth Championships, which were being held in Sherbrooke, Quebec, Canada, in July. I was so excited about representing my country, but little did I know then that there were going to be even bigger fish to fry soon.

The week after the nationals, there was a meeting at Runaway Bay on the Gold Coast. Everyone wanted to run there because it was a fast new track and the wind was always perfect. Given my recent performance, Sharon was sure I'd get a run in the 100m A-race.

She was fuming when we arrived to find I was in the B-race against hurdlers Jana Pittman and Fiona Cullen. I took my anger out on the track and ran 11.57 seconds. It was unbelievable. In the space of seven days I'd slashed .34 of a second off my personal best. In other words, I'd improved by more than 3 metres!

Despite the obvious excitement, there was still steam coming out of my ears as I watched the A-race, which was won by Mindy Slomka in 11.62.

A week later I'd just gotten home after having spent the afternoon playing soccer when the telephone rang. It was Keith Connor.

'Congratulations, you've been selected for the world championships in the 4x100m relay,' he said.

I thought he was talking about the World Youth Championships, because I hadn't officially heard anything about them.

'Okay, thank you.'

And that was the end of the conversation.

I hung up the phone and then thought about the conversation I'd just had with the Australian head coach.

He'd said 4x100m relay at the world championships. The word 'youth' hadn't been mentioned.

Oh my God!

I picked up the phone and rang my coach.

'Sharon, I just got picked for the world championships in the relay,' I screamed down the line.

My coach seemed calmer than I'd expected. 'We already knew, but we weren't allowed to tell you,' she said.

Mum was the next phone call, and she had also been tipped off. Given I was just 16, Connor had wanted to get clearance from her and Sharon about sending me to Paris for the world titles.

'Hang on a minute,' she said when she picked up. I could hear her getting out of her seat and then, in a very loud voice so the rest of her office could hear, she said, 'So, you've been picked for the world championships in the 4x100m relay.'

I was so excited, but there was some drama in the organising. Athletics Australia wanted me to go straight from the World Youth Championships in Canada, which were on 9–13 July, to Europe for a training camp. I would stay there until the Paris world championships started on 23 August.

But Sharon stood her ground. 'She has to come back; she has to keep training and I have to keep coaching her.'

The travelling didn't bother me, as I'd been doing it all my life. When I was three months old, Mum had me on a plane over to England to show off her new baby to the family. I'd also been to Disneyland three times before I was ten because Mum worked for Air Canada, which meant she got really cheap flights. We would often go to England via the US to visit a friend she had in Chicago. Then the stop-off on the way home would either be Disneyland or Hawaii.

Part of being an only child with a single mum was that I learnt from an early age how to look after myself, to be independent and confident in myself. Mum was always telling me, 'You can do anything you want in life.'

She was my greatest motivator, and I knew how proud it made her to see me in my first Australian team jacket. I'd instantly fallen in love with it the moment I put it on at our pre-departure camp. Cameras went into overdrive as we were all so excited to have our Aussie gear on.

I'd decided to do the 200m and 100m hurdles at the World Youths because Sharon and I both agreed it was the best fit on a very tight schedule. It was made tighter by the fact that I also had to do a medley relay, in which four athletes ran different distances of 100m, 200m, 300m and 400m.

What had concerned both of us in the lead-up wasn't so much the hectic schedule, but something that had reared its ugly head during the Australian domestic series.

As part of the 'Talent on Tour' program run by Athletics Australia, a number of elite juniors had been invited to compete at the Grand Prix meet in Canberra. It was a big deal because we were given the same VIP treatment as the star athletes. I went with another Queensland girl, Jackie Davies, and we were picked up at the airport by AA and driven to our fancy hotel, where we stayed the night before the meet. It was my first real insight into the life of a professional athlete, and I liked it – a lot.

Everything had gone smoothly until we were on the blocks for the start of the 100m. This was my first crack at the big time, so I was very toey, and even more so after Jackie broke. Suddenly all I could think about was false-starting. I kept telling myself to stop thinking about it, but as we got into position again, I was scared.

'On your marks, set ...'

I was gone. I couldn't stop myself and left the blocks before the gun.

Given I was the second person to break, that meant I was disqualified. The tears started. I couldn't believe that I'd broken in my first race on the professional domestic circuit.

When I got home, Sharon was waiting with a plan. From that point on, if any member of the squad broke in training, their session was over and they were kicked off the track. She also suggested I speak to a sports psychologist, because every time she'd previously watched Jackie Davies, she'd false-started, and Sharon didn't want me to become like that.

The psychologist was really helpful after I explained how in Canberra I just kept saying: 'Don't false-start. Don't false-start. Don't false-start.'

She told me to turn it into a positive, and we came up with some starting cues that I had to use when I was on the blocks. Instead of the negative slant, I was to now go the other way and say: 'Fast start. Strong start.'

This exercise showed how invaluable it was to have good people around me. Sharon had identified a problem and sought a way to fix it. Having that support base as a young athlete was crucial. So many careers are wasted by not having the right support during those formative years.

The psychologist's advice seemed to work at training, and Sharon's parting words before I left for Canada spelled out loud and clear her thoughts on the matter: 'If you false-start at the World Youths, you're not coming back to this squad.'

I'd always thought
I hadn't done
anything until I
made a senior team.

4

'I'm too tired.' I couldn't believe those were the first words that came out of my mouth after winning my first gold medal for Australia. My teammate Joel Milburn had run down and thrown me an Australian flag because I'd just won the 100m hurdles at the World Youth Championships.

'It's a warm-up lap for the 200,' he insisted.

I smiled, grabbed the flag and did the victory lap. I had the final of the 200m in 30 minutes' time, which was why I didn't think I should be doing any celebrating.

The championships had been madness.

My program had me running seven races in three days, which included three rounds of the hurdles, three rounds of the 200m, and the medley relay.

In the lead-up to the hurdles final, I'd run the 200m semifinal and then the relay heat, where we'd been disqualified because Jackie Davies was in the wrong spot at the changeover.

By the time I got out to the start of the hurdles I was stuffed. I literally sat on the lane box and thought, 'How the hell am I going to run this?'

I actually felt like I was going to pass out for a second. Thankfully, I managed to pull it all together to take the win in 13.42 from Jamaica's Latoya Greaves.

My head was still spinning by the time I got into the call room for the 200m final. I finished fifth in the race, but I didn't really care.

The best part about it all was that Mum had been there to see me win my first gold medal. Her friend in Chicago, Laurie, had surprised her by paying for the airline ticket over to Canada.

Hearing the national anthem and watching the flag being raised was better than I could have imagined, and I actually couldn't stop laughing the whole way through it.

We had six weeks back at home before I headed off to Paris to make my senior team debut. This suddenly meant it was becoming real. I'd always thought I hadn't done anything until I made a senior team.

Mum had instilled in me from an early age not to be cocky or arrogant.

'You've got to stay humble,' she told me over and over

again. I think it was the British way: remain conservative and very polite.

So every time someone would come up to me after a race and say how fantastic it was, I'd always thank them but play it down. I knew I was a good runner but I didn't really count any of it as exceptional until I was going to be a senior athlete.

In my opinion, that's where a lot of kids get messed up – because when they get to their teenage years, they think they rule the world and everything is going to be handed to them on a silver platter. I felt I'd been forced to work pretty hard to get to that point, but the reality was I hadn't achieved anything.

Paris was going to change all of that. But there was one minor issue that I had to deal with: getting in the team. I didn't want to go all that way and not even run. Being the reserve and sitting in the stands was not what I was planning, although we suspected that was what relay coach Cliff Mallett had in mind. Sharon had smelled a rat very early on, as Cliff coached three of the girls in the squad.

Making the 16-year-old the token reserve and getting his own girls in the team was what Sharon thought was the plan.

Ultimately, the result of a run-off – which we'd campaigned for – would decide the line-up. Before I left we put in several weeks of hard training, and Sharon got me to do a time trial against some of my male training partners to get an idea of where I was at.

I was nervous about it, but the result was a pleasant surprise: 11.76. We'd found out the other relay girls, who were already over in Europe at a training camp, had also done a time trial but it had been significantly slower. That certainly gave me a spring in my step when I got on the plane.

There were only three of us flying over together – me, team manager Di Barnes and media manager Katie Hodge – as the rest of the team was already in Europe. We were actually the first ones into the athletes' village – which was in a university compound – and there was nothing really happening there. There wasn't even internet for Katie to do any work, so Di decided to give us a job. We were to travel around Paris and time how long it took from the village to all of the major attractions in what many people call the most beautiful city in the world.

It was a tough gig but someone had to do it, so for the next couple of days Katie and I learnt the ins and outs of the rail system and I quickly fell in love with Paris.

Then all the athletes started to arrive, and I was like a kid in a candy store.

'Oh my God, there's Jana Pittman,' I'd blurt out. 'And there's Tamsyn.'

I had to contain my excitement because, first of all, I had to take care of some important business. Once everyone had settled in, the run-off for the final two spots in the relay team was arranged.

Lauren Hewitt and Sharon Cripps were already in, as they'd qualified for individual events at the championships, so the trial involved myself, Amy Harris, Melanie Kleeberg and Mindy Slomka.

Mallett coached both Kleeberg, who had an injured foot and shouldn't have been over there, and Harris, who was probably the best 60m sprinter I'd seen. Slomka had arrived out of shape, so I liked my chances against her.

I knew I had to smash them so it left Mallett with no wriggle room.

The trial went exactly as expected. Harris flew the start, I quickly took care of the other two, and then with 10 metres to go I caught Harris and comfortably beat them all.

My first visit to the track was on the second day of competition. I went with Mindy, as none of the other relay girls wanted to come out. It was a poor decision by them, because we got to see the most controversial moment of the championships.

It was during the quarterfinals of the men's 100m, and American Jon Drummond protested against being ruled as having false-started by lying on the track and refusing to move. He was adamant he hadn't broken, and for almost half an hour he lay on the track with his hands behind his head, ignoring irate officials.

The crowd were going nuts, first at Drummond, but then, after watching the replay on the big screen, they turned on the officials, as it looked like he hadn't moved at all on the blocks.

I was loving every second of the drama, although it didn't help my teammate Patrick Johnson, who finished last in the race when they eventually restarted it once American team officials had finally convinced Drummond to vacate.

A couple of days later, I was back at the Stade de France. Cripps had made it through the first round of the 200m, but suffered a slight injury and wanted to withdraw from the second round to save herself for the relay. To do that, she needed to go out to the stadium and get permission to compete in the relay. No-one else wanted to go with her, so I was more than happy to get another taste of the electric atmosphere.

This time we had to go underneath the stadium, which meant that after Sharon had got her forms sorted, we got the chance to sneak up through the opening where the athletes walked out onto the track. When I looked up and saw the crowd, I was blown away. There were more than 70,000 people in the stands. It was a goosebumps moment.

Right there and then I made the decision. This was what I wanted to do. This was now my life. I wanted to be at these competitions, in these stadiums, performing in front of all these people.

The heats of the relay were on the Friday, and the night before we all gathered in the basement of our dormitory to watch Jana in the 400m hurdles final. If we needed any more encouragement about what we had to do, Jana certainly provided it when she stormed home over the final 50 metres to win the gold medal. We all went nuts and started jumping around.

I was rooming with Amy, and it was no surprise that we struggled to get any sleep. We were both so nervous that we actually felt sick, as we'd never been to an international meet before, so didn't really know what to expect.

It had been decided that I would run the important final leg mainly because I hadn't been in many relays and they didn't really trust a 16-year-old taking care of a couple of baton changes.

Remarkably, I was calmer the closer the race got. Those nerves from the night before had gone, and when I got out on the track for the warm-up, I took in the crowd, which was doing a massive Mexican wave.

As it went past the top of the straight where the anchor-leg runners were mingling, it hit me. I wasn't in the crowd doing the wave like I normally would be; I was actually part of the show. Then from somewhere in the crowd I heard my name.

'Hi, Sal.'

I turned around and saw a familiar face. It was Matt Favier, who worked at the Queensland Academy of Sport.

'Hey, what are you doing here?' Just seeing someone I knew instantly made me more comfortable and relaxed about the biggest race of my life – which was just about to start.

Being so far away it was hard to tell how we were travelling, although the first change between Amy and Sharon didn't quite seem right and we looked to be behind a few teams.

I was getting the baton off Lauren. The last thing I wanted to do was cause us to be disqualified, but I hadn't heard her yell 'hand', which was the signal to put my arm back to receive the baton.

As I was nearly out of the changeover box – the 20-metre area in which the exchange must happen – I threw my hand back without her call.

It was perfect timing, because almost immediately the baton was there and I was off.

Something strange happened next. I wasn't making up ground. I wasn't catching the girls in front of me.

This isn't right. Why can't I catch these people?

In the end I didn't lose ground, but I was pissed off when I crossed the line in last position. The sloppy first change had cost us and we'd never recovered.

Later, Mum told me how she watched it on TV back home on the Gold Coast, and Jane Flemming, who was commentating, had been impressed with my reaction after the race.

'It's good that she looks really disappointed,' Flemming had said. 'It means she really wanted to win, really wanted to do better.'

I didn't care that I was 16 and was running against some of the fastest women on the planet; I hated losing.

That was the end of my championships – or so I thought. The next morning all of the 4x100m relay girls were called to a meeting with team management. It turned out Jana had pulled out of the 4x400m relay after her victory in the 400m hurdles, and Tamsyn Lewis was also out because of a torn muscle in her butt. They wanted to know if any of us would put our hands up to run. I quickly looked at the floor, because there was no way I was putting mine up.

Then Jana's coach, Phil King, stood up.

'If this was the American team and they were asked this question, every single one of their girls would put their hand up to have another shot on that stage,' King said. 'You should all be very disappointed in yourselves.'

He was making me feel so bad that I felt I had to put my hand up because clearly no-one else was going to.

Straightaway Keith Connor said, 'Don't you dare tell Sharon that you're going to be running the 4x4.'

I didn't understand what he was talking about, but that was mainly because I'd been gripped with fear. I made it out of the room without bursting into tears, but I could feel them building and when I got back to my room I lost it.

'I can't believe I'm doing this,' I said as I sobbed. The whole thing was overwhelming. I was 16, at the senior world championships, and now I was supposed to do a 4x400m relay when I'd never run a 400m race in my life.

Lauren came in to check on me because she knew I was upset, which helped calm me down.

The next morning Keith wanted to have breakfast with me because I think he'd heard I was upset. He didn't really help matters when he pointed out the girls I would be racing against in the 4x400m relay.

'Jesus Christ,' I said. 'They look so big and fast.'

He could tell I was intimidated and, thankfully, after breakfast he made the decision to pull the pin on the 4x400m relay team. I was so happy because it had been a traumatic 24 hours.

It was all forgotten about by the time I got back home to see Sharon and promptly told my coach I wanted to be an Olympian the next year.

'I want to go to Athens for the 100m. I want to qualify.'

She was a bit taken aback.

I knew that in 2004 I'd be stepping up to the senior height in the hurdles – from 76 centimetres to 84 centimetres – and that it would be too soon for me to adjust in time to make the Olympics.

That's why I was pushing the idea of being a sprinter more than a hurdler, because I was desperate for another taste of the big time.

Things had certainly changed, and it wasn't just my mindset. Life was starting to get serious and I even got myself a manager.

My personality meant I always wanted more, whether it was an extra session or just one more run-through.

5

I'd never had my hair blow-dried.

This was one of a number of revelations that took my new manager, Robert Joske, by surprise. As a result I was now sitting in his house in Sydney getting the full beauty treatment. He'd brought in a stylist from Channel 9 to show me how to do my make-up and also select some new clothes.

Fashion certainly hadn't been big on my agenda; my friends and I had all lived in long board shorts and T-shirts at school, and no-one really wore any make-up. Some of my friends started wearing some in Year 10, but I didn't wear much. I mean, before that we didn't even shave our legs, so we were completely out of it.

It certainly felt nice to be pampered for a change, and Robert said it was all part of the process of getting me ready for life in the public eye. That all sounded a bit daunting, but I was happy to again just go with the flow.

The day after I'd gotten back from the World Youth Championships we'd received a phone call from Robert.

'Why do I need a manager?' was my first response to Sharon, when she told me that he wanted to have a meeting.

We looked him up and he certainly had some impressive clients, including Australian Test cricket captain Steve Waugh and Rugby Union star George Gregan.

Robert had received a call from the boss of the Australian Institute of Sport alerting him to my progression, and was asked if he might be interested. The appeal for Robert was that we were starting at ground zero. It was the first time he'd taken on someone at first base, so to speak – his other clients had already been superstars and had come to him for a more sophisticated level of management.

So, given I now had a manager and was a world youth champion, I figured the logical next step was to become an Olympian. My first focus for 2004 was the world junior championships, which were being held in Grosseto, Italy.

The road to the Olympics had gotten harder thanks to a change in the rules regarding the 4x100m relay qualifying. For Athens, they were only going to allow the top 16 nations on times to compete. After a couple of failed attempts, the prospective Australian Olympic relay team gathered at the pre-departure camp being held for the world juniors in

Brisbane. Athletics Australia had put on a meet as part of the camp and decided to send the relay team along for one last attempt.

I was a part of the senior team, but there was to be no fairytale ending again, as we failed to get the baton around. A lot of tears were shed by the four of us because we knew we'd blown it.

Thankfully I had the world juniors to focus on, although my friend Jacinta Boyd, a long-jumper from Queensland who was a member of the 4x100m junior relay team, had a conspiracy theory that I liked. We were on a different flight from the rest of the team and were flying Qantas, the Olympic team carrier, to Italy. She thought that if I ran fast enough and qualified at the world juniors, they were leaving the option of Olympic selection open. While her theory was a bit flimsy, given it was based around which airline we were using compared with the rest of the team, I was happy to entertain it in the back of my mind.

We flew to Manchester first for a competition that was the final hit-out before the championships. I was surprised at how well I ran straight off the plane, clocking 11.60 in the 100m, which was just outside my personal best of 11.57 from the previous year. The relay team also ran well, breaking the Under 20 national record.

The venue for the championships, Grosseto, was in the central Italian region of Tuscany. We stayed at a farm just outside the city. It was beautiful, with this big old house at the end of a long dirt track, although every time you went inside you had to wash all the dust off your body.

I was again competing in three events, with the 100m scheduled before the 100m hurdles and relay. I knew I was in good form as I went 11.60 again in the heats, but come the final I didn't expect what took place.

Generally when you're in the warm-up and then behind the blocks you get a sense of how you're feeling and can predict how the race is going to pan out. I wasn't feeling that great but once the gun went off I ran out of my skin.

It was quick, but when I crossed the line I wasn't sure whether I was in the medals or not. I knew one of the American girls had won but I had to wait for the scoreboard to tell me my own fate.

It was better than I'd imaged. I'd won the bronze medal in a personal best time of 11.40. Ashley Owens from the US had won in 11.13 from her teammate Jasmine Baldwin-Foss (11.34), with little old me third.

My excitement was soon tempered when I realised that in the process of producing a career-best time I'd wrecked myself. I was exhausted when it came around to the final of the 100m hurdles and raced accordingly, hitting a few early hurdles and putting together a poor race. I finished fourth and was devastated. I didn't say a word to anyone as I went through post-event control, and once I got to the warm-up track I threw myself on the ground and burst into tears.

I couldn't believe I'd lost the hurdles.

I was the world youth champion, and I was supposed to be the world junior champion. That was why I was there. That was what was supposed to have happened. When it didn't, I was confused and sad.

My head certainly wasn't in the right space for the relay, but we actually ended up running well for fifth.

Afterwards Jacinta's father, Ray, who represented Australia in the pole vault at two Olympic Games, told me he thought my time in the 100m – which was inside the B-standard on the qualifying list – was going to be enough to get me selected for Athens. (An A-standard time means automatic selection, while B-standard is not guaranteed but makes you a possibility under the selectors' discretion.)

'You wait and see, there should be a letter in the mail for you about the 100m in Athens,' Ray said.

The letter never came.

* * *

It had been a trap for so many, but Sharon was determined it wouldn't happen to me. My personality meant I always wanted more, whether it was an extra session or just one more run-through.

She spent most of her time holding me back.

'You're still just a kid,' she would always say.

I think it was her mothering instinct, because I knew she cared and didn't want me to go down the same road as so many other promising juniors. Sharon has many stories about talented kids she's trained who didn't think they were doing enough, or their parents didn't, so they either went elsewhere and did extra work or did it behind her back.

Every one of them had broken down and ultimately been lost to the sport.

I'd never set foot in a gym until November 2004, the day after I finished Year 12. That was Sharon's rule. Up to that stage I was doing three track sessions and two or three pool sessions a week, plus some core work with the medicine ball.

Sharon's plans for the next 12 months weren't very exciting, but according to her it was a critical time in my development. She called 2005 a building year. My coach wanted me to train through as a senior athlete and build up my strength and fitness for the 2006 Commonwealth Games, which were in Melbourne.

The switch to the high hurdles was a factor, and Sharon went back to Roy Boyd and asked him how long he thought it would take for me to adjust.

He figured it would take me at least two years before I would be able to run under 13 seconds over the higher height.

'Why so long?' was Sharon's response. She didn't believe it would take that long, which I liked, as it showed how much faith she had in me.

I'd recently created a 'goal book', which I would often keep under my pillow, so at any time of the day or night if something came into my head I could write it down.

Having my name in the record books for all of Australia's sprint hurdle records – from junior level to Under 18, Under 20 and open – was now in there in big, bold letters.

The end of my schooling had come and gone without fanfare. Year 12 had been pretty much a joke, given I was hardly there and they only made me do three subjects. My teachers had figured I wasn't going to be doing anything academically, so they made it easy for me. All I had to do was English and two sports subjects.

My progression into life as a full-time athlete was helped by the fact I had my first sponsor. Robert had negotiated a deal with footwear giant adidas, and I was blown away by the fact that they were going to pay me money. I couldn't believe it and I had to keep going back and looking over the figure in the contract – $15,000 per year – to get my head around it.

I was so excited and told Sharon that I could pay for all of us to go to Europe. I clearly didn't understand how much overseas flights cost and soon realised that wasn't the case just yet.

I'd started training six days a week, but that was all I was doing. Mum didn't want me to work because she thought it would tire me and could affect my training. Of course I agreed, but soon realised that sitting around on the couch most of the day wasn't much fun.

The one thing I did do was train hard, and it paid off. My debut in the senior ranks resulted in me getting my own slice of history. I became the first person to double in the

100m and 100m hurdles at an Australian championship, although I was made to work for it by fellow Queenslander Fiona Cullen.

The 100m was first, and I just held on to take the win in 11.77 with Fiona .01 of a second behind. The next day they couldn't split us in the hurdles, and we were both awarded the time of 13.41.

My winning ways continued a month later at the Australian junior championships in Brisbane, where I won the Under 20 100m hurdles by almost 10 metres, clocking 13.84. Everything was on track for the 100m, where I ran 11.82 in the heat to be easily the fastest qualifier for the final.

With my confidence brimming, I was focused on a slick time, given the conditions were perfect with a nice tail wind to assist the sprinters. That was the plan, until about 10 metres into the race when I tore my hamstring.

Previously, when I saw people jump in the air and carry on after tearing their hamstring, I always thought in a way they were faking it. Now I knew they weren't. It seriously hurt. That was the first time I'd suffered an injury of that nature, and I was in agony as I limped off.

The plan was already to focus on training that year, and now we had to throw a few months of rehabilitation into the mix.

Mum certainly jumped onto the program and, as usual, went above and beyond for me. To maintain my body I was going to need massage and physio every week in the lead-up to the Commonwealth Games, which was going to add another $100 to the weekly budget. We didn't have that sort of money, so Mum decided she needed to get another job.

She already worked as a team leader in customer services at trade exchange company Bartercard in Southport. The second job was with the company that took care of the out-of-hours enquiries for Bartercard. It meant Mum worked on the phones from 6 am to 1 pm every Saturday and Sunday, and then one night during the week. It was an incredible sacrifice, working seven days a week just so I could be an athlete. I actually felt guilty about it, but nothing surprised me with my mother.

She'd worked two jobs right up until she was eight months pregnant because she wanted to save up enough money to take me over to England when she was on her maternity leave. For years she'd been baking cakes and selling scones to raise the funds to send me to various junior carnivals around the country. Her boss was a great supporter of mine and it was almost an order in their office that people had to bring in something they'd made at home. Mum would then load up a trolley with all the sandwiches, cakes and biscuits from her co-workers and go around to all the other floors in the building selling the goodies.

Thankfully I lived up to my part of the bargain and was in good shape as I approached the most important couple of months of my short career.

The Commonwealth Games selection trials were in Sydney at the start of February and I went in confident, given I'd run 11.41 at the Telstra A-series meet in Canberra just a week earlier. I was desperate to make my second senior Australian team and didn't miss a beat, improving steadily from the heat to semifinal and then blitzing the final, winning in 11.66 from the Northern Territory's Crystal Attenborough (11.81) with Melanie Kleeberg third (11.82).

There were no mistakes a couple of days later in the 100m hurdles, where I defended my national title by winning in 13.35 from New Zealand's Andrea Miller (13.70).

I was pretty excited when I got back home, although my new boyfriend seemed more surprised. His name was Kieran Pearson, and we'd been in the same year level at high school but hadn't really known each other then. He was an apprentice plumber and gas fitter and not a big track and field fan.

'I'm going to the Commonwealth Games,' I said.

'What, the real ones?'

I smiled and nodded my head. 'Yep.'

'Wow,' he said. 'Are you that good?'

Being at the bottom
of the food chain
like I was meant
you jumped at every
opportunity to get in
competitions.

6

This was the feeling I'd been dreaming about for so long.

I was standing at the finish line inside one of the world's great stadiums, the Melbourne Cricket Ground, with 80,000 people watching me as I looked up at the massive screen.

It had the results of the first 100m semifinal on it:

1. Sheri-Ann Brooks (Jam) 11.35 SB
2. Sally McLellan (Aus) 11.36 PB

The adrenalin was pulsating through my veins. It literally felt like my heart was going to burst out of my chest. And I couldn't stop smiling. I'd just produced the fastest time of my life when it mattered most, on the biggest stage. The energy from the crowd had been amazing and I couldn't wait for when I would be back out there again for the final, in a couple of hours' time.

I quickly made my way through the mixed zone – which was where the media waited to interview athletes after the race – to the warm-down area, where I watched the third semifinal.

In the second semifinal, only the winner, South African Geraldine Pillay, had run faster, so I was eagerly watching to see if anyone else would beat my time.

They didn't.

When I saw Sharon, we hugged and started speaking a hundred miles an hour at each other. I was the third-fastest qualifier going into the final. Suddenly, I was thinking medals.

The Commonwealth Games had already been bigger and better than I could have imagined. I'd been in the first heat of the 100m – it was actually the first race of the athletics program – the previous morning. It was earlier than most people realised, as they'd changed the program to cater for TV, so the stands had been only half full. But it didn't bother me, as I'd won the heat in 11.51.

Now I'd gotten to experience the electricity of a packed stadium, and I was pumped. I didn't want to take the bus back to the warm-up track, so Sharon and I walked back to Olympic Park, which was over a footbridge and down hundreds of stairs. We didn't draw breath the whole way, and by the time we got there it was almost time for me to check in for the final. The runners had to be in the call room 50 minutes out from the race, which was a lot earlier than normal, and then a bus took us back around to the MCG.

There was a small strip of synthetic track underneath the stadium where we could do our final run-throughs. The excitement had been replaced by nerves, and I was actually feeling a bit flat but figured it was just the lull before the storm. I was sure I'd be able to feed off the crowd again.

Everything seemed to be going how I'd imagined it until we were under the starter's orders. I was drawn in lane four, with Brooks, who'd just nailed me in the semifinal, on my inside in lane three.

'On your marks,' the starter screamed.

A split-second later I heard a voice from the crowd.

'Go Sally!'

I was thrown momentarily.

Where did that come from? And why am I thinking about that and not the start?

'Set.'

Then the gun went off.

I missed the start and then stumbled slightly as I got into stride.

What the hell had just happened? I'd been so distracted by someone yelling out my name that I'd completely blown my chances of winning a medal.

As hard as I tried to correct my mistake I was soon reminded that I was no longer racing against other teenagers. This was the big time, and these girls were seriously fast. I pushed with everything I had left but it was a waste of time. I struggled home in seventh position in 11.50. Brooks had won the gold medal in a personal best time of 11.19.

The anguish got worse as I watched the results appear on the screen. Pillay had got second (11.31) with Cameroon's Delphine Atangana third (11.39).

A repeat of my semifinal run would have won me the bronze medal. I was gutted.

I knew I'd just learnt the hard way about the ability to focus. As I walked off the track I made a vow: that was to never happen again.

The good thing was I didn't have long to wait to test my new resolve, as the 100m hurdles heats were in three days' time. There was no way anything was going to force its way through my focus this time, and I got away to comfortably qualify for the final without any problems, finishing third in 13.02, which was just outside my personal best. It was a high-quality line-up, with Jamaica's Brigitte Foster-Hylton breaking the Commonwealth Games record in the heat, clocking 12.65. Another Jamaican, Delloreen Ennis-London, won the second heat in 12.89, while my Australian teammate Fiona Cullen also got through after placing third.

The final was the following night, and the closer it got, the more excited I was because I knew I was going to run something fast, given the perfect conditions and the quality of my opposition.

Whether it was enough for a medal was the big question. Most people thought this was my best chance to do something at the Games, and I really had nothing to lose – which was what I kept telling myself.

I was again super focused when I got out on the track, and didn't let all the noise around me infiltrate my senses. The start to the race was a good one, and at halfway I was in the mix. I knew I had to push, though, if I was going to get a medal.

Then it happened.

I smashed into the second-last hurdle, and from then on it was almost slow motion as I tried to keep my balance – but it was a losing fight.

By the time I got to the final barrier I was on my way down. My shoulder and knee seemed to take the brunt of the fall and for a few seconds I lay on the track in shock. I picked myself up and finished the race in tears.

I couldn't believe I'd fallen in the final of the Commonwealth Games in front of all those people. Then, out of nowhere, my mind wandered back to my first fall at the national high school championships when I was 14. I knew I'd do it again in a final one day.

The tears were quickly getting out of control and I couldn't stop them as Fiona, who had finished fifth, came over to comfort me and help me off the track.

Foster-Hylton had won the gold medal in 12.76 from Canadian Angela Whyte (12.94) with Ennis-London third (13.00).

The media wanted to know what happened but I didn't have an answer.

'I don't even know [what happened],' I said. 'I can't remember. I really don't know what was going through my mind at the time. It didn't turn out how I wanted it to, but that's life. That's what you get for being a hurdler.

'It kills at the moment. My knee and my shoulder and, I guess, my insides.'

They then asked me about the 4x100m relay, which was on in less than 24 hours' time.

'I'm going to go and get ready for the relay. I think we'll do really well in that.'

I sounded confident about the relay with the press, but my body wasn't sharing that same enthusiasm. When I saw Sharon back at the warm-up track, I told her they should get the relay reserve ready because I couldn't even walk up the stairs properly with my swollen knee. The medical staff put me in a wheelie bin full of ice and then wrapped me in so much tape I was like a mummy. Sleep was not going to be on the agenda, as every couple of hours I had to ice the knee and then re-strap it.

When Sharon and team management arrived in the morning, I'd made up my mind.

'I'm running the relay,' I declared. 'I don't care about the knee; I'm not missing out on a medal.'

The pain was bearable and I managed a smile when I saw the morning papers: I was on the front page, my spectacular fall clearly a photographer's dream. It certainly had everything: blood, tears and drama. I was sure I was getting more publicity for falling over than I would have if I'd won.

Thankfully, the ice had done its job and the knee loosened up a lot in the warm-up. I figured the atmosphere in the stadium and the sense of occasion would help take my mind off it for the relay, where I was the lead-off runner.

Getting the baton around without an issue had been a major problem for Australian female relay teams, but I was relieved when my change to Melanie Kleeberg went without a hitch. She passed it to Lauren Hewitt and we were looking good for a medal when Crystal Attenborough took over at the final change.

Jamaica and England had cleared away slightly but Crystal managed to hold down third. Finally, I had my medal.

It was good to have some reward for all the effort. Making two finals at my debut Commonwealth Games was certainly a major positive.

Another was the fact the Australian public now knew who I was – even though it was for the wrong reasons.

* * *

It was the longest three weeks of our partnership. And it was nearly the last.

The World Cup in Athens was the other big event of 2006. Each continent around the world nominated athletes for various events and we were a part of Oceania. I had been selected for the 100m and 100m hurdles.

It was decided we'd do a three-week training block in England beforehand, which would be Sharon's first-ever trip overseas.

Our relationship was at a very interesting stage. Sharon was struggling with the adjustment of coaching a senior athlete, given she'd never done it before, while I was an emotional 19-year-old with a fiery temper. The mix was volatile, and we fought like cat and dog on the trip.

From my perspective the main problem was that Sharon took everything so personally. If I was having a rant on the training track – which was becoming a regular occurrence – I wasn't having a go at her, but that was the way she saw it. Instead of letting me yell and scream, which was my way of letting off some steam, she would always bite back at me, and at one training session she stormed off the track and went and sat in the hire car.

When I walked outside a few minutes later, I saw her sitting in the car. I didn't want to deal with it so I started walking home, but then realised I was a fair way from where we were staying. About halfway I found a petrol station and rang Mum, who'd come over to catch up with her family.

She came and picked me up, and when we got back to the house, my aunt asked, 'Does Sharon know you're here?'

'No, she has no idea,' I said.

A couple of minutes later Sharon was on the phone asking if I was there. The tension between us was uncomfortable, and the trip wasn't exactly going according to plan.

The beauty about being in Europe was that track and field is a mainstream sport there. It was always on TV, and there were competitions going on every second day in various countries. All the best athletes took part in the Golden League series because there was a US$1 million jackpot for any athlete who remained undefeated throughout the six meets. Those who weren't at that elite level were forced to visit the backblocks of Europe in the second-tier competitions to earn a living.

That was where I started.

My first hit-out was in Sweden, where I ran 13.4 for the hurdles and quite enjoyed the experience. The same can't be said about my second competition, in the Czech Republic. I arrived at the airport and was supposed to be met there by someone from the meet. I wandered around and couldn't find anyone until, thankfully, I spotted another Aussie, shot-putter Scott Martin.

I was so relieved to see him.

It turned out he was also competing at the same meet and had been waiting at the airport for two hours. We didn't have any contact numbers or any idea of where we were supposed to be going. Eventually Scott managed to contact Brian Roe, an official from back home who worked as an agent for athletes travelling overseas, and he got hold of the meet organisers to find out what had happened.

One hour turned into five before eventually someone arrived to pick us up. But that wasn't the end of the nightmare, as it was another four-hour drive from the airport to the hotel.

Welcome to the European tour. It was my first taste of life on the road as a professional athlete and I was hating every minute of it. There were two meets back-to-back, with the second in the next town along – which, naturally, was another two-hour drive away.

The ray of light in the whole mess was that I got to race against a seriously good hurdler, American Danielle Carruthers, who won in 12.90. I wasn't far behind her, which gave me some heart.

When I finally returned to England, I'd literally just got off the plane when I got a text from Brian saying a spot had opened up on the start list at a meet in Italy. Being at the bottom of the food chain like I was meant you jumped at every opportunity to get in competitions.

Thankfully, there were no airport issues and the accommodation was great, although I roomed with an Italian athlete who didn't mind being naked in front of me – which I soon learnt was a very European thing.

I came second to Nigerian Josephine Onyia, who'd finished fourth behind me at the 2003 World Youth Championships.

By the time the World Cup came around, Sharon had to return to Australia because of work commitments.

The bonus with the event being in Athens was I got the chance to race in the stadium where the Olympic Games had been held two years earlier. Initially I found it a bit daunting, given some of the names that were lining up in the 100m.

I hadn't done many 100m races in recent times so I wasn't expecting too much, but in the end I was pleasantly surprised with my 11.44 in second-last position. Jamaica's Sherone Simpson won in 10.97 from the American Torri Edwards (11.19).

The Oceania team was producing some good results, the highlight being fellow Aussie Craig Mottram's victory in the 3000m over Ethiopian star Kenenisa Bekele.

I was hoping for a breakthrough in the hurdles, given all season I'd consistently been around the 13.2-second mark, and I knew I was going to need to go faster in this field.

The line-up included Commonwealth champion Brigitte Foster-Hylton, America's Virginia Powell and Sweden's Susanna Kallur, who was Sharon's favourite hurdler because of her smooth style. It was a nice feeling to be behind the blocks with these girls, and I was caught up in the moment when the starter called us into position.

We'd barely got settled when he called 'Set' and then the gun fired almost instantaneously. It was so fast, but luckily I'd reacted better than anyone else. By the fifth hurdle I was still in front, but what I couldn't believe was how far ahead of the field I was.

I knew they would come, and I felt them closing after the seventh hurdle so I just put my head down and kept pushing to the line. When I dipped I looked across and quickly figured out that I'd come fourth, which, given the calibre of the field, was some achievement.

The scoreboard took its time to show the results. Foster-Hylton had won in 12.67 with Kallur second (12.77) and Powell third (12.90). I was sure I was next, and I saw it: 12.95 seconds. Personal best. I started screaming. I'd broken 13 seconds for the first time in my life. I couldn't stop jumping around and when I saw the Oceania team manager, Yvonne Mullins, I asked if I could use her phone.

'Sharon. Sharon,' I was screaming into the phone. 'I just ran 12.95 seconds, Sharon. I did it. I broke 13 seconds!'

She was half-asleep, given it was the middle of the night in Australia.

'Ohhhh, that's so good,' she said.

While we'd had a tough time recently, all that was forgotten in the euphoria of the moment, which I desperately wanted to share with Sharon.

It was strange when I got back to the warm-up track because there were no coaches or friends to meet there. I had no-one to share this amazing feeling of excitement with. I wanted to put my T-shirt over my head and run around like a soccer player after they'd scored a goal.

Breaking the 13-second barrier was so important to me, although it was a double-edged sword. It triggered an obsession that ended up ruling my life for the next six months.

My winning time was the fastest in the world that year ... my goals needed some reassessing.

7

'**I**'m going to break it today.'

Those were the first words to come out of my mouth when I woke up on the second morning of the 2007 Australian championships in Brisbane. I'd never done anything like that before. I was declaring to Kieran that I was going to break the Australian 100m hurdles record.

All season I'd been chasing it, but I suddenly had this strange, overwhelming sense that Pam Ryan's record of 12.93, which had stood since 1972, was going down.

The chase had become a frustrating saga all summer. Every time I stepped onto the track I was asked the question: 'Are you going to break it today?' I'd been agonisingly close on a number of occasions over the previous six weeks, but the weather gods hadn't smiled on me.

In Canberra I'd gone under it, clocking 12.88, but it was with an illegal wind reading of +3.9 metres per second (above 2 metres per second is deemed illegal). I'd also improved my 100m personal best that night to 11.25 – with a legal wind reading – which pushed me up to sixth on the Australian all-time list.

Athletics Australia were doing their bit to help with the record chasing by bringing reigning world 100m hurdles champion Michelle Perry out to compete in the Sydney and Melbourne legs of the domestic Grand Prix Series. Surely, racing against the best in the world would push me under it.

An infected wisdom tooth in the lead-up to the Sydney meet was annoying, but there was no way I was going to miss out on an opportunity to race Perry. The key was not to be overawed by the occasion. I came up with a mantra that I kept telling myself over and over before the race:

I am here because I deserve to be. I am here because I deserve to be.

It worked because I flew out of the blocks and was still leading coming into the final hurdle before Perry effectively monstered her way past. The American was known as a messy hurdler, and I was a bit shocked when she came right over almost onto my lane and her lead arm made contact with me, throwing me off. It was enough for her to get the win in 12.87. My time was again under the record – 12.90 – but the tail wind was too strong at +2.4 metres per second.

Despite the loss it was still pretty nice to be able to say I nearly beat the world champion the first time I'd raced against her. Perry's comments about me afterwards were also heartening: 'I think she's got what it takes. She's got a lot of tenacity.'

The trip to Melbourne didn't go according to plan. I was beaten in both the 100m and 100m hurdles by Perry and was taught a lesson in how to not let conditions dictate performance. Olympic Park had always been a nightmare for sprinters, and I was cranky about the headwinds in the lead-up. It was like I'd convinced myself before the start of the race that the record couldn't be broken. Then when Perry false-started, that threw me out even more. She didn't miss a beat on the re-start, though, and won easily in 12.82 while I ran a horrible race for second in 13.04.

'That sucks,' was my summary of events when questioned about it afterwards.

My last chance to get the record in the domestic season was in Brisbane a week later at the 2007 Australian championships.

The 100m was first, and I was happy to claim my third national crown in another personal best time of 11.23 – the fastest time by an Australian woman in Australia.

Despite waking up the next morning and having my premonition about breaking the hurdles record, I was still very nervous at the warm-up track. Sharon said afterwards that she'd never seen me so stressed – and my mindset didn't improve after some controversy at the start of the race.

When I came out of my blocks, they slipped backwards, so I put my hand up straightaway to indicate the problem to the starter. But by the time he fired the gun a second time to indicate a false start, some of the girls had gone over five hurdles. I couldn't believe this was happening now. It turned out my blocks had no needles in them, which wasn't my fault and I was well within my rights to call a false start.

Once that drama was finally sorted, there was another false start, which thankfully didn't have anything to do with me.

It was a case of third time lucky to get the race under way, and after I'd cleared the first couple of hurdles I knew something good was coming. I felt smooth and fast; the key was to keep it rolling to the end. As I dipped at the line I thought I would be close.

Then I looked up and saw 12.94. My heart sank.

I knew that time was unofficial and it could be rounded down.

'Come on, be nice to me,' I said.

I had my head in my hands as I stared at the clock, and then I heard the stadium announcer say the adjusted time: '12.92.' I screamed the loudest I'd ever screamed and took off on a crazy dance/run routine back up the straight.

Two hundredths of a second! I couldn't believe the clock had done that for me. All the hard work had finally paid off. The monkey was off my back.

Fittingly, Pam Ryan was there to present the medals – but I was taken aback by what she said to me on the dais.

'You shouldn't be aiming for 12.9, you should be aiming for 12.5,' she said.

I was stunned. Here I was, bursting with excitement about breaking the record, yet she was having a go at me.

'Ah, yeah I am.'

When I told Sharon about the exchange she was horrified. The more I thought about it, the angrier I got. Why put me down at such a moment?

I was 20 years old and of course I had long-term goals to go a lot faster, but you also need to have short-term goals, and breaking the Australian record had been it for that season.

Her comments to the media afterwards were also disappointing. 'She was lucky that the start was called back,' Ryan said.

I came away determined to prove that I was more than worthy of holding the record and that in the future I would be going faster than 12.5. This wasn't a one-off. I would show Ryan that this was just a stepping stone to something far greater.

Despite the negative feelings I got from Ryan's comments, the hurdle gods had been on my side, as predicted.

'I told you I'd do it,' I reminded Kieran as we left the track.

The first thing I did when I got home was get my 'goal book' out and put a big tick next to the 100m hurdles open record.

Those goals were done now. What was going to be the next one?

* * *

It felt like I was flying. The ease with which I was covering the hurdles was new. There was a flow that had never been there before.

I'd again started strongly and was in front of two of the best hurdlers in the world, the American duo of Lolo Jones and Danielle Carruthers. This time I was going to hold on. I just knew it.

I did.

As I crossed the line I threw my arms up in jubilation. I'd just won my first international race – but that wasn't all that I was celebrating. The time was out of this world: 12.71.

It had been only two months since I'd broken the Australian record in Brisbane. After chasing that mark for so long I was shocked that in my next race – which was at Osaka's Nagai Stadium in Japan – I'd sliced .21 of a second off it.

I hadn't been expecting it because I came into the race with a badly swollen knee, which had limited my training in recent weeks. Plus I was taking on the top guns. I'd heard a lot of hype about Jones, who'd run 12.56 the previous year, and she'd certainly exuded confidence pre-race. I also knew most of the field had faster times than me coming into the race, but, importantly, I again proved to myself that I could mix it with these girls.

So if they were the best and I'd beaten them – with a bad knee – then why couldn't I be the best? It was a question I was pretty happy to be tossing around in my head.

I did have a chuckle to myself that night as I thought about how Pam Ryan's 12.5 was becoming a reality sooner than we'd expected. My winning time was the fastest in the world that year and, with the world championships back in the same stadium in just over three months' time, my goals needed some reassessing. I'd come to Osaka thinking a semifinal berth in August was about right. I left thinking I could make the final at the world championships.

Even though I was physically exhausted after my career-best performance, there was another opportunity straightaway to race against the same girls at the Doha Golden League meet. I still wasn't used to high-pressure racing, so the more chances I got to put myself in that environment the better. Despite not feeling great, I managed to run 12.90 to finish third behind Virginia Powell and Lolo.

Instead of heading off to Europe and following the tour with the rest of the girls, I headed home, as Sharon wanted to get a solid training block in before the world championships. She still considered 2007 a building year, despite the significant inroads I'd made, and already had one eye on the following year's Olympic Games in Beijing.

The downside of going into a heavy training load was that it sucked the magic of Osaka out of me. Two weeks out from departing for the world championships I was feeling slow.

We had a pre-departure camp in Cairns for the relay team – we'd qualified at the Osaka Grand Prix back in May – which coincided with the North Queensland Games. I ran in the 100m and clocked 11.5. It was rubbish and I was pissed off afterwards.

The reality was that if I served that up in Osaka, my championships were going to be over a lot sooner than expected.

Thankfully, just as the doubts were flooding in, my stubbornness and competitive edge kicked back in.

8

'Run like a final for the first 60 metres and then have a bit of a look and see where you are.'

As usual, Sharon's last-minute instructions were making a lot of sense.

'Then you might be able to slow down.'

My ears pricked up at that. I knew what she meant, but this was my first individual race at a world championships. Could I hold back?

Adding to the case for the negative was the fact that conditions were absolutely perfect. If there was a nirvana for sprinters, then Osaka was it. It was stinking hot, there was a slight tailwind and the track was super fast. Tick. Tick. Tick.

The heats of the 100m were on the second morning of competition, and I felt confident there would be no repeat of the Commonwealth Games issues. This went up a level once I got down into the blocks and felt the heat off the track. Everything was perfect.

As was my start.

In what seemed like a blink of an eye I was already at the 60-metre mark. It felt amazing; I was smooth and seemingly doing it with ease.

'Sorry Sharon', I thought.

The last thing I wanted to do was stop this feeling of pure speed that I was experiencing, so I kept going through to the line.

As I dipped I noticed someone a few lanes across, but what really caught my attention was the clock: 11.14.

What the?

I was stunned. That was a massive personal best and it brought me within a whisker of a record I'd circled long ago – Melinda Gainsford-Taylor's Australian record of 11.12, set back in 1994.

It only took about a minute before the excitement was replaced by distress. I was so hot. Every part of my body seemed to be burning. I managed to make it over to the mixed zone where the Australian journalists were waiting for a comment about the second fastest 100m by a woman in the country's history.

'It's so hot,' I said, before collapsing to the ground in front of them. I felt like I was going to pass out, but team

ABOVE: With my mother, Anne, when I was just a few weeks old.
MIDDLE LEFT: Proudly showing off my monkey bar skills at the age of one. Mum says this was the moment she decided I was going to be a gymnast.
BELOW: My fourth birthday party with friends from left to right: Samantha Judson, me, Amanda Judson and Scott Hulbert.

ABOVE: My first day at Coogee Public School with Samantha Judson. BELOW: After competing in the Queensland Schools Athletics State Championships in 1999. We won the 4x100m relay representing the South Coast region and I'm in the blue singlet at the bottom next to Dana Feltcher.

ABOVE: At the opening of the Couran Cove Resort on South Stradbroke Island where I got to meet my hero Cathy Freeman. BELOW: I was so excited to meet Cathy and was lucky enough to get her autograph on my cap – she was so inspirational and I really wanted to be like her.

LEFT: Competing in the 100m hurdles heats during the IAAF World Youth Championships on 11 July 2003 in Sherbrooke, Canada. I was 16 years old and it was my first international event. (Photo by Michael Steele/Getty Images)

BELOW: When I won the 100m hurdles at the IAAF World Youth Championships on 12 July 2003 in Sherbrooke, Canada. It was a thrilling moment to be winning my first gold medal in a world event.

(Photo by Michael Steele/Getty Images)

ABOVE: Competing against Ashley Owens of the United States (740) who won the women's 100m final from Jasmine Baldwin (709) second, and I won bronze at the IAAF World Juniors Championships on 14 July 2004, in Grosseto, Italy. (Photo by Michael Steele/Getty Images)

BELOW: Winning the women's 100m race during day two of the Athletics Australia Telstra A-series National Championships at Sydney Olympic Park Athletic Centre on 5 March 2005. (Photo by Mark Dadswell/Getty Images)

ABOVE: I was devastated when I fell during the women's 100m hurdles final at the Melbourne 2006 Commonwealth Games. Brigitte Foster-Hylton of Jamaica won gold, Angela Whyte of Canada won silver and Delloreen Ennis-London of Jamaica won bronze. (Photo by Stu Forster/Getty Images)

BELOW: The 4x100m relay team of Melanie Kleeberg, me, Lauren Hewitt and Crystal Attenborough are thrilled to learn we have won a bronze medal in the Melbourne 2006 Commonwealth Games. (Photo by Mike Hewitt/Getty Images)

ABOVE: Representing Oceania at the World Cup in 2006 at the Athens Olympic Stadium where I finished fourth in the 100m hurdles and broke the 13-second barrier for the first time.
BELOW: With my 4x100m relay teammates at the World Cup from left to right: me, Melanie Kleeberg, Fiona Cullen and Preya Carey.

ABOVE: Priscilla Lopes-Schliep of Canada, who won bronze, celebrates with me after I won silver in the women's 100m hurdles held at the National Stadium on day eleven of the Beijing 2008 Olympic Games.
(Photo by Jeff Gross/Getty Images)

LEFT: Another big moment in my life was my wedding day in April 2010 when I married Kieran Pearson.

doctor Tim Barbour grabbed me and immediately started putting ice packs all over my body.

My mind and body had played tricks on me because, while the race felt so easy, clearly I'd worked incredibly hard and was now paying the price. I had no energy. My body was on fire, and somewhere in the back of my distressed mind I thought about how I had to come back in nine hours' time for the 100m semifinals. And the following morning I had the heats of the 100m hurdles.

Right there and then I made a decision. There was no way in the future I was going to do two events at a major championships; it was simply madness.

Eventually, after more ice treatment and truckloads of fluid, my body temperature came down, but I was still so tired. How I even made it back to the track that night and then managed to qualify for the semifinal by running 11.31 is beyond me.

I was actually a bit scared about what I was going to be asked to do out on the track in the next 24 hours, given how spent I was physically. Thankfully, just as the doubts were flooding in, my stubbornness and competitive edge kicked back in. It was time to click into 'go with the flow' mode, which I'd done so well as a junior, because the bottom line was that I'd signed up for all this. It was too late to stop, so there was no use complaining.

To put a positive spin on it, you could say I was 'in the zone' when I arrived at start line for the hurdles heat, but it was more like a daze. Despite seven hours' sleep, I still felt fatigued. I was in the opening heat at 10.10 am and I'd been so wrapped up in my recovery the previous night that I hadn't even noticed that reigning world champion Michelle Perry was in my heat. All I knew was I was in lane nine.

My hip flexors and abductors were still suffering from the personal best in the 100m, but I knew there could be no holding back given the fast conditions that were again on offer.

Being in the outside lane meant I couldn't get a feel for the rest of the field, so I just had to do my own thing. My start was poor by my standards, and it was hard work from then on. It felt like I was in a final rather than a heat, and the time suggested that – 12.85, which was the second fastest of my career. I'd finished second behind Perry, who ran 12.72, and the times in the other heats were also super slick.

But I had to quickly switch off hurdle mode as the 100m semifinal was next on the agenda in the evening session.

My aim coming into Osaka had been to make the semifinals of both events, so anything from then on was a bonus. The problem with that was that when I was on the start line, I just wanted to compete and beat them all. That's what I'd done in every race I'd ever run. I didn't care who it was next to me; I always thought I could win.

Once again I started well, but it was soon apparent that these girls were in a different league and I finished last in 11.32. The winner, America's Torri Edwards, ran 11.02 while the other semifinal was won by Jamaican Veronica Campbell in 10.99.

I soon realised this experience was invaluable, looking ahead to the 2008 Beijing Olympics. And at 20 years of age, I was in the top 16 sprinters on the planet.

My schedule had come in for some criticism at home, with Sharon's daughter, Richelle, ringing her up in tears after my hurdles heat.

'You have no idea what they're saying on television about you,' Richelle said to her mother. 'It's so mean and terrible.' Apparently Jane Flemming had teed off, saying I was going to be burnt out and was receiving bad advice.

Sharon wasn't concerned. She kept telling me I didn't have to make any decisions yet because I was still a baby in terms of athletics. And I'd always said to her that I loved the freedom of running the 100m and the challenge of doing the hurdles. We both knew a decision was looming, but for now my challenge was to find a way to qualify in the hurdles semifinal.

I was going to have to go under my personal best of 12.71 to make the final. Every race had been so fast in Osaka that I was confident, despite having raced so much, that this could be achieved. But what's that old saying about biting off more than you can chew? Unfortunately, that's what happened in the semifinal.

Despite starting well, it was soon obvious that it wasn't there. Perry won in 12.55 and I finished fifth – one spot from progressing through to the final – after clocking 12.82. Doing five races in three days had finally gotten to me.

The media were keen to find out which event I would be focusing on in the future, but I wasn't ready to make that call.

'I am learning now, unfortunately, after I finish my races,' I said. 'I have learnt not to do two races at these sorts of events. Now I know what the feeling is like to run at a world championships in a 100m and a hurdles, so next year at the Olympics I will choose one event. It will be very hard and very emotional but I will choose one event, where I am higher ranked and running better in.'

I'd managed to hide my frustration about missing out on the hurdles final quite well in front of the press, but as I walked back to the warm-up track with Sharon, it boiled over. The tears started to flow and Sharon started getting angry at me for being upset.

'Just let me be angry,' I screamed.

Again she was taking things personally. I wasn't angry at her or blaming her for what happened; I was just disappointed with how I'd gone in the hurdles. Sharon couldn't see that and, given how fried I felt, it was a volatile mix.

* * *

'No, it's just not good enough.'

And with that I turned on my heels and left the television interviewer and my teammates with their mouths wide open.

I was fuming.

We'd just finished second-last in the heats of the 4x100m relay, and yet when the other girls spoke afterwards they'd said it was a 'good effort'. I was seeing red, and my anger was mainly directed at one person: Melanie Kleeberg.

I'd been the lead-off runner with Melanie at second change, which had been a disaster. She took off way too early and had to slow down dramatically just to be able to accept the baton before then having to get going again. After she passed it to Crystal Attenborough, I pulled up alongside her and screamed, 'You took off so early. I can't believe you did that.'

Crystal passed it to Fiona Cullen, who then crossed the line in eighth spot in a time of 43.91. Belgium had won the heat in 42.85.

After the blow-up in the interview, Melanie confronted me.

'You embarrassed your country by going off and being angry,' she said.

I tried to calm myself down, but was struggling to hold it in.

'I was being truthful about how bad our team just ran,' I said. 'That sort of performance is not going to get us anywhere.'

The difference between my mindset and that of the other girls disturbed me greatly. We were mentally at completely different levels. I couldn't understand why they were just happy to be out there wearing the Australian uniform. I wanted to get through the round. I wanted to make the final. I wanted to get a medal. I wanted to be the best in the world. It's why I hated running relays. I was pleased when the biomechanical data came back on the relay and justified my spray, as it showed Melanie had taken off 4 metres early.

I was weighing up whether to head back to Europe or go home when I got the call-up for the hurdles A-race at the biggest Golden League meet of the year in Zurich. Initially I had been the reserve, but American Virginia Powell pulled out so I was elevated into the main event.

But I had one question: 'How much prize money does the winner of the B-race get compared to last place in the A-race?' I was told the B-race winner took home US$4000.

It didn't end up mattering, as I ran really well in the A-race, clocking 12.74 to finish fourth behind Susanna Kallur, who'd turned the tables on Perry.

Perry had won her second world title in Osaka, clocking 12.46, but Kallur – who finished fourth in a personal best 12.51 – felt she'd been interfered with by the American in the final. Her revenge on Perry in Zurich was sweet, given the defeat meant the world champion was no longer eligible for the US$1 million jackpot at the end of the series.

I was just happy I'd earned more than US$4000 for my efforts. I still remembered how excited I was when I got my first prize-money cheque – it was a few hundred bucks for finishing third in the 200m at the Melbourne Grand Prix.

When I finally got on the plane for home, I had all the confidence in the world looking at what the next 12 months had in store. While I was still quite immature and didn't properly comprehend the world of professional athletics, I'd learnt so much throughout 2007. I'd been in races and situations that, at such an early stage of my career, I'd never dreamed of being at.

Bring on Beijing.

In the space
of an hour, my
whole outlook
had changed. The
doubts about my
fitness and form had
vanished.

9

My coach ran one hurdles race in her life.

Sharon enjoys telling the story about how she was a 13-year-old schoolgirl at St Monica's College in Cairns, and no-one else in her sports house would have a go at the hurdles. The race was on a downhill track, and she still came last.

It always gets a laugh out of me, that story, because generally in most sports the elite coaches have played the particular game at the highest level. That's the tradition, particularly across the football codes in Australia, but it wasn't an issue in our case because Sharon knew more about hurdling than any hurdler I'd ever met.

She spent hours and hours analysing footage of me and my rivals, searching for the most minute technique changes that could improve my race by a fraction of a second. When Michelle Perry was in Australia, Sharon never put down her video camera. She was so excited about getting to see close-up how a world champion operated. 'If you want to be like the top girls, you've got to do what they do,' she would say over and over again.

At the start, my technique was terrible. When you first start hurdling, the greatest barrier is fear. It's human nature that your mind sees the hurdles and instantly calculates the safest way to get over them to avoid injury. This isn't the fastest way, and getting to the point where you're not scared of the hurdles and are able to throw yourself at them is the key.

As you can imagine, this takes a long, long time. When I started I always thought that my lead leg – the one that goes straight out at the barrier – was always going to go underneath the hurdle, which would mean crash time. The mind plays serious games with you, and the only way to build confidence is by practising the same thing over and over and over again. What became really frustrating was that I got to the point where I knew I wasn't scared anymore, but I just couldn't get my leg to go straight. Much to Sharon's frustration it kept hanging out there or, as she put it, my lead leg 'went west'. She estimated it was 35 degrees west, and it took us years to get it back heading straight towards the finish line.

When people ask my coach about the intricacies of hurdling, she says the easiest way for her to explain it is to get out her photo album. Inside, she has pictures of me hurdling every year from the age of 15. The progression in my technique every 12 months was incredible. But every year Sharon seemed to have a new area to fix. Recently we'd looked at my arms and upper back position. I'd also started plyometric training – a series of jumping exercises in short explosive bursts – because to maintain the right technique over 100m you needed strength in every part of your body.

The bottom line is that hurdles is a rhythm event, and it isn't just about being able to run fast. For Beijing, I'd decided to continue seeking that magical rhythm. In the end it was actually an easy decision when Sharon and I sat down and looked at the world rankings in the 100m hurdles and 100m. At the end of 2007 I was ranked equal 11th in the hurdles and 25th in the 100m. Given my expected rate of improvement in the hurdles, it wasn't going to take much to get in the mix, whereas such leaps in the 100m were clearly going to take a lot longer.

Now all we had to do was get ready for the Olympic Games. And that made us both nervous.

* * *

Something was wrong.

I couldn't shake this feeling that I was going to tear my hamstring. It was weird, because it was like the premonition I'd had before I broke the Australian record 12 months earlier.

I was getting more and more anxious in the warm-up as I prepared to run in the heats of the 100m at the 2008 Queensland championships in Brisbane. Normally before a race I can picture what sort of time I will run, and I can visualise the actual race and finish. Today there was nothing. I couldn't picture anything. I watered down my fears with Sharon.

'My hamstrings are a bit sore,' I said.

She figured it was related to a back spasm I'd had a week earlier that had forced me to pull out of a 200m race at the Australian Athletics Cup in Canberra.

I hated not competing and my stubbornness kicked in. Sure I was just being silly, I decided to run the 100m. Halfway through the race I realised I hadn't been silly. The hamstring grabbed and I pulled up. I was so angry at myself as I hobbled off. I'd torn a hamstring before so I knew all the dangers, but I hadn't listened to the warning signs. With the Olympics just six months away, I couldn't afford to make those mistakes.

Thankfully I'd started the Australian season the way I'd wanted, which had given me great confidence. On 12 January at the Sydney Track Classic, I'd produced the fastest hurdles run on Australian soil: 12.81. That showed I'd already gone up a couple of levels from the previous year, and, importantly, that was the type of time the best girls opened their seasons up with, so I was very happy.

Two weeks later in Canberra, I was surprised to find myself even happier. I'd run the 100m first and won in 11.41, but it had felt bad. My legs seemed like they didn't want to move.

'Everything hurts,' I said to Sharon.

As a consequence my expectation for the hurdles race an hour later greatly diminished. I was wrong. From I don't know where, I ran 12.72, just .01 of a second outside my personal best.

'I was feeling like crap,' was how I described the race afterwards.

Given I was running 12.7 in January, we figured I would improve down to at least 12.5 at the Olympics, and that would put me in the final.

Then my stupid psychic premonition came along and I blew out my hamstring, which ended all those warm and fuzzy thoughts about Beijing. The injury meant I missed out on the two major meetings on the domestic calendar in Sydney and Melbourne, where I was set to race against Jamaican sprinter Sherone Simpson, who was the fastest woman the world in the 100m in 2006.

I was also a no-show at the Olympic selection trials in Brisbane from 28 February to 1 March. That wasn't a drama as I'd already qualified for Beijing, but it meant more time in the swimming pool than the running track. The pool had been a constant since I'd fractured my foot years before, and I'd been Sharon's guinea pig in many ways as she experimented with what the body could and couldn't handle in the water. It took a lot of sessions to get my pool fitness up, and many times I almost passed out beside the Southport pool because of the extreme amount of lactic acid in my system.

Sharon would constantly be yelling at me: 'Boil the water up. Boil the water up.'

At the start I had no idea what she meant, or what good could come from all this exercising in the pool. 'Boiling the water' involved lifting my body up by turning my legs over quickly underneath the water and then lifting my elbows out of the water in a sprinting motion. That caused the water to splash around, which was how Sharon came up with the 'boiling' imagery.

I could only do it for a few seconds at a time initially before I slowly mastered it and came to understand the benefits, particularly in helping to build up strength in my arms and legs. Sharon was sold on it and would later describe it as our secret weapon.

* * *

Diamonds are a girl's best friend.

I'd heard the saying before, but had never really gotten the chance to embrace it until there was an unexpected turn of events in Switzerland.

I was kicking off the crucial final phase of my Olympic preparation with a 100m hurdles race in Lucerne. My hamstring recovery had gone according to plan, so much so that I'd already had a brief hit-and-run mission to Europe; Sharon had been concerned about how far advanced I was with my training and decided I needed to race, so in June I went over for the Golden League meetings in Berlin and Oslo. I wasn't sure about the idea and my concerns were valid, given my performances.

In Berlin I'd finished seventh in 12.94 behind Spain's Josephine Onyia (12.50). Five days later in Oslo there was only a slight improvement, coming in sixth in 12.87, again behind Onyia (12.59). I returned home with my tail between my legs, but Sharon was confident that with another month of training the wheels would start to turn.

That was hopefully going to happen in Lucerne, given there was just a month to go until the Olympic Games. I had no idea what to expect, although the bonus was the presence of 2004 Olympic champion Joanna Hayes in the field.

What happened in that race left me gobsmacked. I not only beat Hayes, but I also smashed the Australian record, clocking 12.58.

The race felt very weird. It was like I couldn't keep up with my legs; they were going so quick that I had this sense that I was going to topple over. I'd experienced a similar sensation in Osaka the previous year, when I made the breakthrough from 12.9 down to 12.7.

My agent, Maurie Plant, was in the stands, and as soon as I crossed the line I saw him standing up going crazy. Immediately, I sensed my perspective change. Before that race I'd been stuck running 12.9 or 12.8, which wasn't going to get me anywhere in Beijing. But this time made me a legitimate contender.

I was on cloud nine as I warmed down, and then Maurie yelled to me from the stand.

'You're up for the diamond,' he said.

I had no idea what he was talking about. 'What?'

'You could be about to win the Diamond Jackpot.'

I quickly sacked the warm-down and went over to get more information. It turned out the meet was sponsored by a diamond company, and they were trying to build up the meet's profile by offering a one-carat diamond, worth US$15,000, for the performance of the night. This was judged on world rankings, and my 12.58 had rocketed me up the charts to number eight.

Maurie explained that the only danger for the diamond was Brazilian pole vaulter Fabiana Murer, who was still competing.

My Australian teammate Alana Boyd was in the event, so I rushed over and sat next to her father, Ray. Suddenly I was more nervous than I'd been before my hurdles race. Every time Murer was on the runway I was whispering, 'Miss. Miss. Miss.'

She'd cleared 4.70m, and the next height was for the meet record, which, if she nailed it, would earn her the diamond. After two misses I almost couldn't watch the third attempt. When I saw the bar topple, I let out a muted 'Yeeeessssss.'

I'd never *seen* anything worth so much money before in my life, let alone held it in my hands. The diamond was tiny but beautiful, and I knew it would fit perfectly in a ring to mark a special occasion down the track! In the space of an hour, my whole outlook had changed. The doubts about my fitness and form had vanished. I was now excited and pumped about what lay ahead.

The London Grand Prix was next, and the favourite was Lolo Jones, who'd produced the fastest time for the year – 12.45 – just three weeks earlier at the US Olympic selection trials in Eugene, Oregon.

For the first time I was really enjoying being in the spotlight next to the likes of Jones. And with my confidence up, the best part of my race again came to the fore. I flew out of the blocks and was in the lead at halfway. By the seventh hurdle I was still in front and I knew I was running out of my skin.

Then I hit the last hurdle and stumbled badly. I managed to stay up, but literally jumped over the finish line as I was still off balance and figured I might as well get in the air rather than hit the ground.

Despite smashing the hurdle, stumbling and jumping over the line, I still finished second to Jones and ran 12.61. The American had only beaten me by .03 of a second, so I must have been a long way in front coming to the final barrier. What pissed me off more was that I'd clearly been on track to smash the Australian record until I'd made a mess of the tenth hurdle.

I got another chance three days later in my final race before the Games, in Monaco. The most exclusive principality in the world was as glamorous and beautiful as I'd imagined. On the morning of the meet, Sharon and Ray Boyd got me and Alana, who was also competing at the event, to come with them to visit the palace. We took off on what we thought was an easy stroll up the hill. It was a bad miscalculation, as the trip took a lot longer than we expected and the day was getting hotter and hotter.

As spectacular as the palace was, finding a cool drink was the focus once we made it up there. I was starting to get a bit anxious, but that was offset by the fact that the stunning weather meant conditions were going to be perfect for the race later in the evening.

And they were.

The track had a reputation for being fast, and the stillness in the spectacular Stade Louis II had my adrenalin pumping. This was a perfect opportunity and I was determined not to stuff it up.

I didn't.

The Australian record was broken for the second time in two weeks as I clocked 12.53 to finish second behind Jamaican Brigitte Foster-Hylton (12.49).

I was on a roll just ten days out from the start of the Beijing Olympics.

You've beaten these girls before, you've done this a million times. You know how to hurdle; just go out and do it again.

10

'Who deserves to be the gold medal favourite for the 100m hurdles?'

I was seated at a table inside the dining room of the Hong Kong University with a bunch of Australian journalists around me.

'Me,' I said.

They all started laughing, but I was only half-joking.

'Whoever wins it, they deserve it, obviously, because they did it on the day,' I continued. 'Hopefully it's me. I'll be happy with anything for the final. I wouldn't be happy if I didn't make the final.'

The 100m hurdles was more open than normal, and I was now the fifth fastest in the world in 2008. Athens champion Joanna Hayes didn't make the US team, nor did Michelle Perry, the two-time world champion. Another top American, Virginia Powell, was injured, as was Perdita Felicien, the Canadian who won the 2003 world title. And Susanna Kallur from Sweden, the silver medallist behind Perry in Osaka 12 months ago, was running injured.

'It's going to be a very tight race,' I again emphasised to the media contingent.

We were all in Hong Kong because the Athletics Australia officials, in their wisdom, had decided this was the venue for the Olympic team's camp on the eve of the Games.

It was a dump.

I wasn't as upset as many of the others because I just thought it was normal for teams to stay in small dormitories with hard beds and flat pillows. Pole vaulters Steve Hooker and Paul Burgess left because they deemed it unfit to stay in and went to a friend's apartment elsewhere in Hong Kong. I didn't know Hooker at this stage and initially I thought it was prima donna behaviour, but I soon appreciated why he'd done it. To become the best in the world you had to look after yourself the best way possible. And this was far from the best.

What had infuriated many was the fact that the distance runners got to stay in a five-star hotel in another section of Hong Kong because the university didn't have any running trails for them to train on.

I was too excited to be overly concerned, although what had me upset was the fact that we'd been banned from going into Beijing for the opening ceremony. The reasoning was the expected high levels of pollution – which didn't eventuate – were going to harm our preparation and affect our ability to perform at our best.

It was a joke, and to make matters worse, they made us attend a function in Hong Kong with some businesspeople where they had the opening ceremony being shown on a big screen. As I watched the other athletes walk into the incredible 'Bird's Nest' stadium, I suddenly burst into tears.

Why wasn't I there?

Instead, I was stuck at the back of the function room by myself until 400m runner Joel Milburn came and sat with me.

Olympic team manager Geoff Rowe had told us the people at the dinner were potential sponsors and that we were to be nice and speak to them, but that was the last thing I wanted to do. I don't know if it was nerves about what was coming up, but I was very emotional and, unfortunately, what should have been a memorable evening became truly forgettable.

* * *

The laundry service blew my mind.

While there were so many things that had my head spinning about the Beijing athletes' village, simple things like someone doing your washing made me so happy. The fact that you could put your washing in a bag, drop it into the laundromat and then come back in a couple of hours to pick up the finished product was the highlight.

That was closely followed by the size of the cafeteria, which was the biggest room I'd ever seen in my life. To walk from one end of the Olympic Village to the other took half an hour, which shows how big it had to be to house the 16,000 competitors during the Games.

Playing the waiting game was never much fun, and I decided not to go and watch any other sports, preferring to wait for the track and field to start. Plus I didn't want to take any risks with my back, which had played up in Hong Kong. Because I had strapping all the way round my waist, which made me walk funny, I'd actually been smuggled past the waiting media at the airport when we arrived in China. They got Tamsyn Lewis to go out ahead of me and keep the cameras amused while I quietly slid past and got on the team bus. It worked a treat.

The back issue meant I was certainly on edge at training. Sharon and I had our regulation little spats as the tension mounted, because I wanted every session to be perfect, given the biggest event of my life was just days away.

My roommate in the village was heptathlete Kylie Wheeler, which turned out to be a problem. While she was a lovely girl, Kylie was a serious snorer. I'd noticed it at the start but it hadn't really annoyed me, but the night before my first race, that changed. Naturally your senses are a bit wired on the eve of a race at the Olympic Games, so the snoring became a major issue. Early in the morning, it got to the point where I had to leave the room and sleep on the couch in the lounge room.

Tamsyn, who was running both the 400m and 800m at the Games, found me. 'What are you doing?'

'I'm sleeping here because Kylie is snoring.'

Without another word, Tamsyn burst into the room and told Kylie to get out.

'Sally is sleeping in the lounge because of you,' she said. 'You have to leave so she can go back to bed.'

I didn't want to make a scene, but Tamsyn was on a mission. My roommate was very apologetic as she crept out, and I managed to get a couple more hours after she'd left.

The hurdles competition was spread out over three days instead of two, which was a bit unusual, and meant extra tickets had to be bought by my support crew.

Mum and her friend Vicky – I had done Little A's with her daughter Sonia and they'd become good friends – plus Kieran were there for my first Olympic Games.

All the controversy in the build-up to the Games about the pollution turned out to be unfounded, given the conditions inside the incredible stadium were ideal for sprinting. We knew the track would be fast, and Usain Bolt showed that on the second night of competition when he smashed the 100m world record, running the unbelievable time of 9.69 seconds.

Sharon wasn't part of the Australian team management so she was staying away from the village, which meant she had a daily battle with the Chinese transport system. That was an adventure I knew she could have done without.

She was able to get access to a personal coach accreditation, which got her into the warm-up track. Team management gave her an ill-fitting Australian uniform so she would look the part.

I was calmer than I'd imagined for my first race at an Olympic Games – mainly because I think I was relieved that it had finally arrived. But all the waiting around in the village was draining, and it seemed like ages since I'd raced in Monaco. Despite this, I felt more than ready to get underway as I lined up in the third heat of the 100m hurdles.

That changed the moment the gun was fired.

Everything felt weird, and I was all over the place throughout the race. It was almost like I'd forgotten how to hurdle. It was the worst I'd run for months and I finished second in 12.83, a whisker behind Jamaican Delloreen Ennis-London (12.82).

I was a bit shocked, but at the same time I knew the heats were all about getting through to the semifinals. I'd done that, so I had to move on and forget about it. That was easier said than done, and I woke up the following morning like a bear with a sore head. Everything was frustrating me as the nerves hit about the semifinal.

'Are you okay?' discus thrower Dani Samuels asked as we sat in the lounge room of the apartment.

'Not really,' I answered carefully through gritted teeth. 'I'm not really in a good mood.'

Dani's response was perfect. She started laughing, which helped break the ice.

By the afternoon I'd started to feel better. I now had a sense that everything was going to work out. It wasn't as clear as my previous premonitions, such as when I broke the Australian record, but all of a sudden I was a lot more positive.

My goal was to make the Olympic final, and to achieve that I had to qualify in this race. I'd warmed up brilliantly, which helped the situation, but I was more serious than usual as we gathered behind the blocks.

I could hear people in the crowd yelling, 'Go Sally. Go Sally.' I had no idea who they were and barely acknowledged them as I attempted to zone in. I had to get this right.

My job was made a lot harder by the fact I was out in lane nine. That meant I wouldn't have much of an idea what the rest of the field were doing, which was a problem, given only the first four progressed through to the final.

I started well, but again my technique felt rusty. Approaching the final hurdle I sensed I was up there, but when I dipped and looked across there were too many in my line of sight for my liking.

A sense of dread came over me. I'd blown it.

Lolo Jones had won in a personal best time of 12.43, but there were a bunch of us together over the line next. The scoreboard was taking forever to figure out the placings and finally it was there: 'Sally McLellan 12.70 q'.

That little letter 'q' was all I needed to see, and instantly I felt a massive weight lift off my shoulders.

'Thank God,' I said aloud to no-one in particular. I was into the Olympic final. I'd finished fourth, with Ennis-London second in 12.67 and Priscilla Lopes-Schliep third (12.68).

As I passed through the mixed zone, I was informed that I was only the third Australian to make the Olympic final, joining Pam Ryan (fourth in 1972) and Glynis Nunn (fifth in 1984).

That was nice to know, but there was more history to be made.

* * *

'How do you do this? What do I do?'

I'd plonked myself down next to Bronwyn Thompson, who was having lunch in the village cafeteria. My fellow Queenslander had been in my position four years earlier when she made the long jump final at the Athens Games. She'd finished fourth, and what she said to me hit home.

'At least you're not Cathy Freeman at the Sydney Olympics on the starting blocks,' Bronwyn said. 'You don't have that sort of pressure on you, so you can just go out and enjoy yourself. Relax, because you can only control what you can control. Do what you normally do, remember what it's been like in Europe and do the same thing. You've beaten these girls before; you've done this a million times. You know how to hurdle; just go out and do it again.'

I felt like jumping the table and giving her a big hug. Everything she said made sense, and from that moment on I was a different person. I'd been lost and pacing the room in the morning; now I was excited about competing again.

Sharon also seemed relaxed – or at least she was doing a good job of hiding her nerves – when we met up to go to the warm-up track.

It was chaotic in there, with people regularly wandering across the track where we'd set up three hurdles to practice.

Craig Hilliard, one of the Australian team coaches, and Sharon had to get help from some British and Canadian officials to build a human wall around the hurdles so I could do my reps without the danger of cleaning someone up.

Ennis-London was next to me, and she looked to be really flying.

'That's so fast,' I said to Sharon.

'You're faster than that.'

I stopped and looked at my coach. 'No, I'm not.'

Sharon was adamant. 'Yes, you are.'

'How do you know?'

'Because I've just seen it with my own eyes.'

These momentary doubts regularly kicked in at this stage, and I went over to Craig for a second opinion. He was just as positive, and when I went back for my final run-through, I was telling myself not to be scared of the hurdles. Over and over I said that as I pushed hard.

When I'd finished I went back over to them and stated my intentions.

'I just have to really gun it.'

We all walked together over to the call room with Craig talking about the TV show *The Simpsons* for some reason to try to keep all of our minds relaxed.

When we got there, Sharon stopped and gave me a big hug and said, 'This is it, Sal. No guts, no glory.'

I started to act strangely while we waited underneath the stadium. I was talking to myself – a lot. I'd never done that before, and now, bizarrely, I wasn't even scared to say things out loud.

'C'mon,' I said in my best Lleyton Hewitt impersonation as I stepped out onto the track.

For some reason as I took off my top after my final practice run, I was convinced I was going to be on the dais. I wasn't thinking about winning, and for some reason bronze wasn't hitting a chord in my psyche either.

As the starter called for us to get into our blocks, there was a calmness about me. I was in lane three, on the inside of Lolo.

All year I'd nailed my start and I was clearly the best at it in this field.

Attack the first hurdle. Focus on your own lane.

I went almost simultaneously with the gun – the official reaction time was 0.138.

That is the best start of my life.

I was clearly in front over the first hurdle and was still there over the second and third.

Just keep going. Just keep going. Just keep going.

Over the fourth hurdle it dawned on me.

Shit, I'm winning the Olympic Games!

I knew something special was going to happen when I was still in front over the fifth hurdle, but as I approached the sixth I felt something.

Oh crap, here we go. They're going to come over the top of me.

By the seventh Lolo had clearly headed me.

Just run your own race. Run your own race.

Then it happened. Lolo hit the eighth hurdle and almost fell.

Oh my God. GOOOOOOOOOOOOOOOO!

I didn't want to be distracted by what had happened, because previously I'd lost concentration during races and it had cost me.

Don't look at her.

As I got over the final hurdle I realised I had no idea where anyone else was.

It's the Olympic final; have a look.

I turned my head to the right as I started to dip for the line and couldn't believe what I saw. There was only one ahead of me. The rest were just behind. I'd done it.

SILVER!

Instead of slowing down I kept running towards the big screen.

Where's my name?

Dawn Harper had won the gold medal in 12.54, but there still wasn't anyone else's name up there.

I'm going to run up there and do it myself if you don't hurry up!

It was the longest 90 seconds of my life. Then the screen flickered: 2 – Sally McLellan AUS 12.64.

I am an Olympic silver medallist!

I started squealing and jumping up in the air. I grabbed hold of Priscilla Lopes-Schliep and we just screamed at each other.

The reason for the delay was the fact that she had the same time as me and they had to go to 1/1000th of a second to split us – 12.632 to 12.633. Only two hundredths of a second separated second and sixth. Lolo had finished seventh.

I saw Dawn take off on her lap of honour and realised I needed an Australian flag. There certainly hadn't been any prior arrangement regarding a flag, given no-one thought I was going to be needing one.

All of my teammates were seated back at the start of the 100m, so they couldn't help, but luckily a random person out of the crowd threw one down onto the track.

I draped it over my shoulders and bounced around the Bird's Nest. It was an amazing feeling to see the crowd standing and clapping. At the 200m mark it hit me. The tears started to flow, and they were still going when I saw Mum, Vicky and Kieran waving frantically at me.

I went over and gave them a big hug.

'It was magic,' I kept saying over and over again.

By the time I made it back to the finish line I also had a green-and-gold pompom to go with my flag.

I was still in shock when Pat Welsh from Channel 7 grabbed me for an interview.

'Oh my God, you have got to be kidding me, right?' I said. 'Is this real? It's amazing, I can't believe it. I don't know what to say … Can you believe it? Did you see me at the start, did you see how pumped I was? I was more pumped than I have ever been in my life. I wanted it that bad.'

I was babbling as I tried to comprehend what had just happened. I'd barely made it through the mixed zone when officials ushered the winners into a small room where we waited before going back out into the stadium for the medal ceremony.

The three of us were laughing and giggling the whole time as we tried to put our tracksuits on, but it was so hot and sweaty, which made it almost impossible to do. Priscilla had forgotten her pants and she was supposed to wear black, but ended up borrowing her team manager's, even though they were red.

When I walked out to the dais and got the silver medal around my neck, I thought about a book swimmer Brooke Hanson had written called *When Silver Is Gold*. That was exactly how I felt. I felt like I'd won.

It was rare to see all three medallists so excited together, and as we posed for a photo the announcer was moved to say, 'And look how happy all of them are.'

That was certainly the case, although when we were on our way to the press conference, for the first time I felt something different. Dawn was showing us her gold medal and I was envious. I suddenly felt like I really wanted that medal.

After clearing all my media commitments I finally made it back to the village, where my celebration was a cheeseburger from McDonald's.

I then ran into Bronwyn, who again seemed to know what I was thinking.

'Did you feel slightly funny towards Dawn and her gold medal?' she asked. She'd been the only person who'd thought of that.

'Yes,' I said slowly, 'yes, I did.'

She knew I could have been an Olympic gold medallist – and I knew, the next time, I would be.

The problem had been that I thought I was invincible ... I just thought I could do anything.

11

I slept with the silver medal around my neck.

When I say 'slept', it was only about a 45-minute nap, as there was no way my mind wanted to rest; it was still racing. I had a bizarre moment when I woke up and looked at the medal. For some reason I thought it was fake, and for a few seconds I didn't understand why I was holding it.

I quickly snapped out of it.

I'd done it. I'd shocked everyone by winning it, and I loved it so much. There were more interviews arranged, but the highlight of the day after was finally getting the chance to catch up with my coach.

Sharon was simply proud, and explained how she had an Australian flag over her head during the delay in the placings coming up on the screen, because she couldn't watch.

We had a proper celebration that night at the China Doll nightclub, which was where all the athletes went to party, and I danced up a storm.

It was back to business soon after, though, with more races in Europe before I'd get the chance to head back to Australia and show off my silver medal.

The first was in Zurich, where I finished third (12.63) behind Lolo Jones (12.56), but the more interesting race was in Brussels. I hadn't run very well, and at the finish line I was looking up at the screen, which had my name in third position with a time of 12.84.

Lolo had finished second (12.67) to Delloreen Ennis-London (12.65) and she was right next to me when I said, 'That sucked. It was a really bad race.'

'What did you say to me?' she said in an aggressive tone.

'I meant I ran bad.'

'No, you said something about me in the papers. Something about you wanted my scalp.'

I was stunned. 'What are you talking about?'

She walked off, but the conversation continued at post-event control when we were getting dressed. I asked again what she meant, and she suggested maybe it had been my coach who'd said I wanted her scalp.

'What's wrong with that, Lolo?' I said. 'It just means I wanted to beat you.'

'Well, don't say that because it's horrible.'

I felt like she was taking this way out of context. It was only later that I realised that the phrase would have been offensive to her, given her Native American background. At the time, though, I thought she was being unreasonable.

'Seriously, just chill out Lolo.'

My heart wasn't in these races, although it was worth the effort financially. I was just going through the motions and finished fifth in Zagreb in 13.02, the slowest time I'd run in years.

At the World Athletics Final in Stuttgart I again struggled home in sixth (12.82), with Lolo taking home the big prize money on offer, with victory in 12.56.

I was much happier to be taking home an Olympic silver medal. The reaction back in Australia was an interesting one. Most people wanted to tell me how hilarious I'd been in the post-race interview. Apparently it had been one of the funniest things they'd all seen. I wasn't sure if that was a good or bad thing, as I didn't want people to make fun of me. I'd just been reacting in the moment, and I think they all understood that.

For the first two months after I got home I was the busiest I'd ever been, zipping off to functions all around Australia. It was an exciting time because I'd obviously never done anything like that before and it was almost like I was being treated as royalty. I couldn't help but wonder what it would be like if I'd actually won gold.

The success in Beijing also saw my bank balance grow, which was exciting. There were bonuses from the sponsors I already had on board, and more wanting to get involved.

Everyone kept asking how my life had changed after winning an Olympic silver medal. What it did was let me live in the house I was going to buy, rather than having to rent it out. There was no Olympic letdown.

When it was time to get the spikes back on, I was more than ready. I was actually training so well at the start of 2009 that a trip to the US in February was added to my race schedule.

I'd never run indoors before, but I liked the sound of spending time in New York and Boston. The first race was a 60m hurdles event in the Big Apple, and I loved exploring one of the best cities in the world. I'd always enjoyed just grabbing hold of a map and looking around, although others often didn't share my sense of adventure.

The other Aussies who were competing at the event, including pole vaulters Steve Hooker and Paul Burgess, preferred to sit in cafes and drink coffee.

I did make a bit of an error with my walk through Central Park, as I didn't have the right clothes or footwear for the wet and slippery conditions. Added to that was the fact that my luggage hadn't turned up for three days, so I had to wear the same clothes – which I'd managed to get soaking wet.

My agent, Maurie, had more to complain about, though, after an unfortunate fall. We were training at a university just past the Bronx and had gotten off the bus to go in when he slipped on a massive piece of ice and hit the deck.

I was literally half a metre behind him, so I was very lucky. He ended up in hospital with a broken rib.

The meet was at the famous Madison Square Garden, and I was very apprehensive about the whole indoor thing, as it was quite different from anything I'd experienced. First, I had to get my head around the fact that there were only a few metres from the finish line to the wall, where you had to crash into a massive cushion to stop your progress.

The Americans also liked having tape across the finish line, and I was totally distracted by that in the race and ran the last couple of metres with my hands out in front of me to break it. With all that going on in my head, I still managed to finish just .01 of a second behind Priscilla Lopes-Schliep.

Boston was next, and I met Mum's friends from Chicago there, which was good, although it was bitterly cold. Snow was everywhere, so going outside wasn't a great idea. We did manage to make it to the Cheers Bar, and I also trained at Harvard University, where they gave me a free T-shirt, which I was pretty happy about.

This time I was racing over the 60m flat, and I soon learnt that it didn't allow you much time to make up for any mistakes.

My first two strides weren't great, and from there I was in trouble. I finished sixth behind American Lisa Barber

(7.19), but the time of 7.30 was good enough to break the 22-year-old Australian indoor record.

The most exciting part was yet to come with Hooker, who'd won the Olympic gold medal in Beijing, becoming the second highest vaulter in history when he cleared a remarkable 6.06m. It was incredible to be there to witness such a great performance from a fellow Australian.

The good news when I got home was that some talented internationals were coming out to take part in the domestic series. American sprinter Brianna Glenn and Jamaican hurdler Brigitte Foster-Hylton would be my rivals, which was a major boost for my preparation, which was aimed at the world championships in Berlin in August.

My heat run at the Queensland state titles told Sharon and me that we were well and truly on track. I cruised to the line, clocking 11.26, which was seriously quick for early in the season.

After winning the 100m hurdles at the Sydney Track Classic in 12.84, I came up against Foster-Hylton in Melbourne a week later, where I managed to prevail in tough conditions, winning in 13.06. I also took out the 100m, running 11.56 to defeat Melissa Breen, with Glenn third.

The national championships were in Brisbane, and I again took out the double, winning the hurdles in 12.74 and the 100m title in 11.32. My confidence couldn't have been higher, and instead of following the same competition schedule as the previous year, I suggested to Sharon that we mix it up. The theory was that we'd competition-hop through Europe rather than have a specific base. I wanted to stay in all the glamorous cities and enjoy life following the Golden League circuit.

It was a bad move.

* * *

'Let's go one-two at the worlds this year.'

Priscilla Lopes-Schliep was excited. We'd just crossed the line at the Monaco Grand Prix, and it had been fast. I'd just done exactly what I'd done 12 months earlier at the same track: break the Australian record. Importantly, I'd also won the race in 12.50 – it had initially shown 12.49, but unfortunately was rounded up – with Priscilla second in 12.54.

'Oh yeah, for sure,' I said.

The second I said it, this feeling of dread came into my mind. I wasn't going to get a medal at the world championships.

What the hell? What is my mind doing?

The problem was that my track record with these bizarre hunches had been good in the past. I should have been dancing around, celebrating the fastest time of my career, but instead I felt tired and sore. All I wanted was some physio and a decent massage.

Monaco had been my fifth race in three weeks, and it was taking its toll. I'd won four of the five, against all of the best girls going around, so on all the evidence I was the one to beat in Berlin.

But something wasn't right. I had to front up again three days later in Stockholm, but on the morning of the race I wanted out. I'd never felt like that before. I was a competitor and had never walked away from a race, but I was exhausted and my hamstring was tight.

A sure sign that all wasn't well was when I left my race numbers back at the hotel and Sharon was forced to go back and get them. Normally I was always organised hours in advance before races, so that just made me more anxious about the situation.

There were heats before the final, which wasn't always the case on the European circuit. This usually didn't warrant a second thought, but halfway through my heat I started to go backwards. It was weird, but luckily I still managed to get third and progress through to the final.

But that excitement just wasn't there, and I struggled into fourth (12.64) behind Priscilla (12.51), who just defeated our good friend Lolo (12.52).

Lolo had missed out on a spot on the US team for the world championships after she fell in the semifinals of the trials. Unlike Australia, the US had cutthroat trials, with the first three across the line getting the gig. Lolo had the fastest time in the world that year, 12.47, and I was next on the list, which was why everyone was talking about me as the favourite in Berlin. The problem was, I felt anything but like a favourite.

And it was about to get a lot worse.

* * *

The run-through was one I'd done a thousand times before.

It was the last one of the set, and I wasn't even at full pace when suddenly I experienced a sharp pain in my back. I screamed out and crumpled to the ground straightaway. It was like I was paralysed. Sharon came running over and tried to help me up, but I couldn't move.

We were in Cologne, Germany, at the Australian team's pre-departure camp, just two weeks out from the world championships.

A couple of days earlier I'd had a back spasm while I was on the massage table, but it was nothing compared with the pain I was experiencing now. I was freaking out, and whatever the physio was trying to do seemed to make it worse. Everyone was panicking and I was in tears. I kept asking, 'Why now?'

Eventually the team doctor managed to calm everyone down. He ordered me to do nothing for a week, and he was going to get special exemption to prescribe some heavy-duty medication to accelerate the healing process.

'How am I going to win now?' I kept asking Sharon. Sadly, we both knew the answer to that question.

Every day I was in tears, and for the first 72 hours after the mishap, I was bent over on a 90-degree angle like a grandma when I walked. I even needed assistance just to get out of bed. The way I was feeling, I was going to be lucky just to make it onto the track for the first round.

In hindsight I knew we'd made some errors. Going away from the previous year's program and doing so many races without medical support had been a disaster. The problem had been that I thought I was invincible; after winning the silver medal in Beijing and then hitting the ground running so fast in the new season, I just thought I could do anything.

What I'd failed to do was look after my body. For the first month in Europe, I didn't have access to physio or massage treatment. Now I was paying the price.

As the days went on, the more I was getting myself worked up. The pressure of the whole situation with the injury and the expectation that came with being the favourite was getting to me.

I needed to talk to someone who knew what I was going through, and there was only one person I could think of: Cathy Freeman. I'd been lucky enough to be given her email, so I figured I had nothing to lose if I asked my idol for some advice. I explained my situation and how I was actually thinking about the cutthroat semifinals in Berlin, and not even the heats, which was very odd.

Cathy, who'd won two world titles before her Sydney 2000 success, was quick to reply and said she could relate to my feelings. It turned out in the lead-up to the 1995 world championships she couldn't even go to the toilet without thinking about racing.

'Take a few deep breaths and enjoy the moments when you're not racing,' Cathy wrote. 'Enjoy when you can relax and just be yourself.'

On the seventh day of the recovery process, I was allowed to do a pool session under strict supervision by the medical staff. I did another one two days later, and that was it. That was my preparation for the world championships.

My back was still sore when I boarded the Australian team bus to head into Berlin. The next dilemma we faced was whether to tell anyone about my condition. My instinct was to not let my rivals know I was injured. I was still holding out for a miracle, so I didn't want to give them any indication that I was vulnerable. But I also understood the argument that telling the media would take the pressure off, given everyone in Australia expected me to win when I could hardly move.

Team management were divided. Head coach Eric Hollingsworth wanted it kept in-house, while Craig Hilliard had the opposite view. I wasn't going to lie, but after long discussion I decided it wasn't in my best interests to volunteer the information. This theory was put to the test when I was one of the main drawcards at an adidas press conference.

By that stage my mindset had changed. The injury had happened, and now I had to deal with it, get on with the job and race.

'When the world championships come around you just get your head down and get on with it,' I told the assembled journalists. 'I'm ready to race and do what we came here to do.'

Steve Hooker was doing a good job of running a distraction for me, given he was also under an injury cloud, but the difference was everyone knew about it. He was having daily press conferences to update his condition, so that helped reinforce in my mind that I was doing the right thing.

Two days out from the start of the championships I managed to run again, albeit rather gingerly. I was banking on the adrenalin kicking in on race day, and while I may have been injured, the competitive spirit still pumped through my veins.

It kicked in when I had a look at the IAAF official program for the championships. For each event there was a list of seven contenders for the gold medal. I wasn't even mentioned. That was enough to get me at least a little fired up for the heat, which I managed to win in 12.82 from Ireland's Derval O'Rourke (12.86).

The semifinal and final were just 90 minutes apart the next night, which made Sharon and me very apprehensive. If it had been like Beijing and spread over three days, that would have been ideal to manage the injury, but going back to back was going to make it a lot tougher.

There were three semifinals, with the first two placegetters in each automatically qualifying, plus the next two fastest. This was all I could think about halfway through the race, because Dawn Harper was leading and I was having all sorts of trouble getting past Jamaica's Lacena Golding-Clarke, who was on my inside. She was beating me all the way up to the final two hurdles, where I had to dig deep just to make sure I got through to the final.

I'd been forced to push all the way, and had one word for Sharon afterwards: 'Horrible.'

That also described my warm-up for the final. My back was stiff again, and I was in a fair bit of pain as I tried to do some light jogging. It was a case of fingers crossed as I went into the call room for the final. I sat down at the back, and all I could think about was getting the race out of the way. I didn't want to be a part of the world championships anymore. I was sick of everything.

Then Priscilla came up to me and recalled our conversation from three weeks earlier in Monaco.

'We're going to go one-two,' she said with a smile.

'I'm just happy to be here,' I said.

She looked at me strangely. It wasn't the attitude to have 30 minutes out from a world championships final.

When we got out on the track, my biggest challenge was to just be able to execute over a couple of hurdles in the warm-up. I hadn't done anything since the semifinal, so when I got over the first hurdle without incident, I looked up to where Sharon was in the stand and she punched her fist.

It was almost like I'd won the race.

The start of the final was delayed because Germany's Robert Harting had won the men's discus gold medal and was going crazy celebrating. His victory lap was one of the slowest in history, and the longer it went the more I felt my focus was slipping. I found myself getting really distracted, which was the last thing I needed given I was up against the odds anyway.

At least I started well from lane seven and seemed to be keeping up with Priscilla on my inside for the first half of the race.

I was right in the mix coming into the seventh hurdle, but then it happened. My fitness gave way. That missed training block was coming back to haunt me.

Priscilla had pulled away from me and when Delloreen Ennis-London, who was on my outside, edged past I was gone.

I lost concentration and hit the final hurdle, stumbling over the finish line.

Jamaica's Brigitte Foster-Hylton had won in 12.51 from Priscilla (12.54) and Delloreen (12.55). I wasn't even next, with O'Rourke, who'd never gotten close to me before, finishing fourth (12.67). I had finished fifth in 12.70.

That upset me as much as anything. She would not be allowed to beat me again. I was emotionally drained by the time I walked off the track and felt like just going away and hiding from the world.

The problem was that the media wanted an explanation for my disappointing performance. 'I pretty much cried myself here. I had a pretty bad back injury. I couldn't even get up without assistance, so it wasn't the best week before the worlds.'

'It's been hard to deal with but I got here and I got to the final, that was my main goal. Unfortunately I ran the best that I could with the little amount of training I have done.'

I was hurting, and it got a lot worse when I learnt that the front page of *The Age* newspaper back in Australia had run an article calling me a liar for not revealing the injury.

That was the final straw.

I'd also finally come to the realisation that I had to stop blaming everyone else. Once I did that, I was able to look forward.

12

'I can't do this. I can't be here right now.'

And with that I left Sharon in the grandstand of the Gold Coast Athletics Track and walked away. For how long? I wasn't sure. The way I was feeling, I had no intention of returning. I was depressed.

After the dramas in Berlin, Kieran and I went on a holiday around Europe, but I beat myself up the whole time. I went running every day, which I think was some form of punishment of myself, given I hadn't done enough when it mattered a few weeks earlier. When we returned home, things just got worse. I was in all sorts of pain, mentally and physically.

I didn't want to see the track; I didn't want to see Sharon or have anything to do with my training partners. I was wounded, and every day it hit me. The tears would generally come while I was hiding away at home. There were demons in my mind that weren't going away.

After weeks of ignoring all attempts to lure me back by Sharon and others, finally I saw a light at the end of the tunnel. And it came from the most unlikely source: heptathlon.

I needed to do something different to get me back to the track. I'd toyed with the seven-discipline event as a junior, and figured it might be a bit of fun. We pencilled in my heptathlon debut for a Gold Coast interclub meet in November.

The doctors had given me the all clear to train for it on the proviso that if my back played up again I would ditch it. We'd had scans done when I returned from Europe that showed I had a tear in one of the lower discs. The doctor said I was lucky to get up for the world championships final, because most people wouldn't have been able to walk with that injury.

My new event was certainly going to test out the body, given a lot of different muscles groups were required. The javelin throw was interesting and I could only get it 25 metres, which wasn't great, while I was doing my best not to think about the 800m.

Unfortunately, I didn't have to bother, as just a couple of weeks into the heptathlon training my body told me it wasn't a good idea. Sharon had played along because it had gotten me out of my funk and at least back at the track. The problem was the track was still making me miserable, because every time I was there my back hurt. It was a vicious circle. A boot camp in Cairns at the end of 2009 with the rest of the squad was Sharon's suggestion as a circuit-breaker.

I wasn't a good person to be around up there and was blaming everyone around me for what had happened. The demons were coming out, but by the third day I was glad I'd made the trip.

In the end I actually enjoyed throwing myself into some hard training, which included a lot of running up hills and stairs. I also finally came to the realisation that I had to stop blaming everyone else. Once I did that, I was able to look forward.

The big carrot in the distance was the Commonwealth Games, which were being held in Delhi, India, in October 2010.

'I want to win the Commonwealth Games,' I declared to Sharon, who was taken aback by my statement. It was the first time as a senior athlete that I'd said I wanted to win a particular race. Given the Games were late in the year, there was plenty of time to get back into shape.

Thankfully I had a new job to keep my mind active and happy: wedding planning. Kieran and I had set a date for 3 April 2010, so there was plenty to be organised. It was certainly the most enjoyable job I'd had since I left school – and there had been a few that had been tried and tested, then ultimately ditched. I'd worked in the mailroom at Mum's work for ages, which had to be the most boring place in the world. A couple of years previously I'd done a fitness course at the TAFE, but hated it. I was with all these gym junkies who thought they knew everything, and it was essentially a waste of six months.

My first love was animals. We had a beautiful Golden Retriever called Oscar, whom I adored. I actually think I like animals more than humans, and my dream is to work with them later in life. I'd already done some volunteer work at the Currumbin Wildlife Sanctuary, and it was something I was going to look at when my career was over.

Right now, though, I had to focus on getting my career back on track. Three weeks of pain-free training had helped leading into the first major meet of the 2010 domestic series in Sydney.

I had no idea how I was going to run, and I knew I had a legitimate challenger in Melissa Breen, who'd shown early in the season that she was in good shape and improving as a sprinter.

My prediction about Breen was right, as halfway through the 100m race I was in trouble.

She was leading, and my first loss in more than four years was suddenly staring me in the face. Then the competitor in me kicked in. I knew I didn't have the fitness or the training behind me, but there was no way I was going to lose this race. But even after I pushed over the final 20 metres and dipped at the line, I thought I'd come up short.

I looked up at the scoreboard, and it had my lane number

next to 11.39. I couldn't believe I'd won, let alone run that fast, given the shape I was in. It was the shot of confidence I needed, and there was more to come when I backed it up and won the 200m in 23.19, which left Sharon shaking her head. She was at a loss to explain how, in my first hit-out since the world championships, given everything that had gone on over the past six months, I'd produced those times.

It was so good to be feeling happy about running again, to have that love of the sport back. And that was why I did something I'd never done before: I pulled out of a race.

I didn't want that good feeling to be deflated, so I withdrew from the 100m at the Melbourne Grand Prix because I was convinced Breen would beat me. I told the race director that I was doing it so I could focus on the 200m, where I was seeking a qualifying time for the Commonwealth Games. The reality was I'd only prevailed over Breen by .01 of a second in Sydney, and I didn't think I had another performance like that in me at that stage.

It was a preventative measure, but I didn't want my newfound confidence to be splattered all over the place. Breen went on to win the 100m in 11.41, while I took out the 200m despite the poor conditions in 23.55.

The Commonwealth Games selection trials were next, but I was giving them a miss for a more important event. I was walking down the aisle at the Royal Pines Resort on the Gold Coast.

Everything had gone according to plan, and I had a special surprise for everyone. My family knew about my love of classic movies – I had cupboards full of them at home – and my favourite of all time was *The Wizard of Oz*.

In honour of Dorothy from the movie, I wore a pair of bright-red glittery shoes underneath my traditional wedding dress. It was the perfect touch for the best day of my life.

* * *

I'd never been so happy finishing third.

My first race back in Europe was at one of my favourite tracks, in Monaco, on 22 July, and I was so excited to have that feeling of speed again.

I'd been nervous coming into the Diamond League meet and had actually asked my agent, Maurie Plant, how much prize money was paid for last place.

But I got out of the blocks well and was actually winning at the halfway mark. Then I felt Lolo Jones come up to me and, with a couple of hurdles to go, Danielle Carruthers also went past. That didn't bother me as much as it would have previously, and I was happy with third in 12.76.

We'd delayed coming over to Europe for as long as possible because the Commonwealth Games weren't until October. That still meant we were looking at a three-month stint overseas and, unlike the previous year, we decided to base ourselves in Cologne.

Athletics Australia booked a two-bedroom apartment for Sharon and me – Kieran was staying at home to get his business off the ground – but it turned out not to be what we'd expected. There were certainly two beds – but they were a metre apart from each other.

For nine weeks that was our living set-up, and it was no surprise that it put a strain on our already volatile relationship. Sharon was still running a business back home, so each night she'd be on her computer while I tried to sleep.

'Stop clicking,' I would yell at her constantly.

Sometimes she'd hide in the toilet with her computer so I wouldn't be disturbed.

It was tough going, and it didn't help that boredom was also a major issue. The facilities for training were ideal – the track was good and the gym was excellent – but there was nothing to do. I ended up counting down the days before each trip to the next race.

My next event on the Diamond League circuit – which was the renamed Golden League – was in Stockholm. After running 12.70 and finishing third in the heat, I produced my best performance for a long time by winning the final in 12.57 from Priscilla Lopes-Schliep and Lolo.

The wheels were starting to turn and I kept up the momentum over the next month by running consistently around the 12.6 mark. This was a huge breakthrough, because previously I'd been more up and down with my speed.

Priscilla was the form runner, and it wasn't even frustrating me that I kept finishing second because I was just glad to be back in a positive frame of mind.

The Continental Cup – which had previously been known as the World Cup – was the main goal for the European trip, and it was being held in Split, Croatia. I was super excited, and it wasn't just because of the $30,000 winner's cheque. The prospect of getting away from the gloom of Germany to the sun and heat of Croatia had me counting down the hours until we arrived.

My excitement at the change of venue may have been over the top, because I strangely found myself feeling horrible in the lead-up to the race. We hadn't lightened off the training yet, as the Commonwealth Games were still a month away, so I figured that was why I was flat.

The one thing that did fire me up was the presence of Lolo Jones in the field. I hated losing to her and that was what I was using as motivation in the minutes leading up to the start. It worked.

Much to my surprise, I put together an excellent race and just clung on. I took the win for my team, Asia-Pacific, in 12.65, with Jones second in 12.66.

The afterparty was at the hotel where we were staying, so I took the opportunity to let my hair down for the first time in a long while. Everyone was buying me drinks and there was lots of champagne getting thrown around.

The highlight, though, was my first Tim Tam for months, thanks to my teammate Jody Henry's mum, who'd brought them over with her. I was in heaven.

Unfortunately, I was snapped out of it the next morning because I had to return to Cologne. We were only there for another week or so, as Athletics Australia had committed to an 'Ashes'-style showdown against the British in a street meet in Gateshead. The bonus was that the organisers were paying for three weeks' accommodation for the Australian team at the Hilton Hotel.

While the change of scenery was good, it was bitterly cold. Sitting around in 3-degree weather wasn't exactly ideal preparation for the Commonwealth Games, which were going to be in 35-degree heat in India.

I managed to win a 150m event at the Ashes, but the best thing to come out of Gateshead was a change in my plans for Delhi. It came about after a training session I did with some of Australia's best male sprinters, Aaron Rouge-Serret and Matt Davies. Sharon wanted me to do some starts with the boys, and each time I beat them over the first 10 metres before their strength would kick in and they'd catch me.

'I think you should do the 100m in Delhi as well,' Sharon said after the session. 'You need another focus and some sort of excitement.'

Up until then we'd only been looking at 100m hurdles, because of the lessons learnt at the 2007 world championships.

'Are you sure?' I said. 'Do you really think so?'

The program at the Commonwealth Games was better set out to do both events, so I welcomed another challenge and the prospect of another gold medal.

* * *

Given how I'd felt in the semifinal, I was excited about what time was possible in the 100m final. I'd been revitalised by the heat of Delhi, and it had helped me turn a blind eye to the horrendous conditions we were dealing with.

We'd arrived at our apartment at 2 am, and it was the most disgusting thing I'd seen. There were faeces floating in the toilet, and the showers were also putrid. They also told us not to go out on the balcony, in case it fell down.

After lots of scrubbing and disinfecting, our living quarters became bearable and I enjoyed the Commonwealth Games. My performance in the 100m semifinal added to my happiness, given I'd jogged the final 15 metres, looking around, Usain Bolt–style, and still clocked 11.28.

The plan was to smash it in the final. That was all I was thinking about on the blocks – clearly a bit too much, given what happened next.

For the first time in years I predicted the gun rather than waited to hear it. I knew straightaway I was out. After one stride I put my hands to my face as the second gun went off to signal the false start.

I couldn't believe I'd made such a stupid mistake.

The new start rule meant there were no longer any second chances: if you broke, you were out. I didn't want to look up at the official whose job it was to walk over to my lane with a red card to signal my disqualification. After a few seconds there was nothing. Where was he?

I looked up and saw that he was in front of lane four, which was England's Laura Turner, and he had his red card pointed at her.

It turned out we'd both gone early, but the timing system showed she had gone first by .0001 of a second. Turner refused to move, and argued she'd been disturbed at the start. After several minutes it was decided she could run on protest.

I couldn't believe I'd dodged such a major bullet, and there was no way I was going early off the blocks again. In fact, it ended up being one of my slowest starts for a long time – which meant I found myself fourth at halfway. But I was building momentum, and with 10 metres to go I came over the top of race leader Nigerian Oludamola Osayomi.

Even when I'd crossed the line I still didn't allow myself to celebrate until I saw my name up on the big screen; given what had just happened, I was taking no chances. This time I had nothing to worry about. I'd won the gold medal in 11.28, and now it was time to celebrate.

With an Australian flag draped around my shoulders, I took off on a victory lap around the Jawaharlal Nehru Stadium. My post-race TV interview was a bit more controlled than the one in Beijing.

'It is so unbelievable because of what happened,' I said. 'I thought I was out, and then it was Laura who got the disqualification red card. Then all of a sudden I came out and won the race.'

I couldn't wait to get my hands on the gold medal. It was my first title, so I knew it was always going to hold a special place in my career. The ceremony was scheduled for shortly after the race, so officials escorted the medallists quickly to a waiting area. As we started to walk back out into the stadium, there was a flurry of activity ahead before an official ordered us to stop. They wanted us to go back inside.

'Why?' I asked. 'What is going on?'

I couldn't get a straight answer from anyone before finally one of the chief officials said there had been a protest. He couldn't tell me who it was against, but said that the medal ceremony was off until it was resolved.

I didn't understand. They'd ruled it was the English girl who'd broken, and she'd actually finished last in the race anyway, so I didn't think there would be a problem. I was getting more and more anxious as I searched for Sharon or any Australian official who could shed some light on this bizarre situation.

Eventually head coach Eric Hollingsworth found out what had happened. England had lodged a protest over the start, but it wasn't to help Laura Turner, whose disqualification had been upheld. They wanted me gone as well, so then it would elevate another English girl, Katherine Endacott, from fourth into the bronze medal position.

The longer it dragged on, the angrier I got.

After a couple of hours we were told the IAAF appeals jury had upheld England's protest. The Australian team management immediately fired in a counter-protest, given the data showed it was Turner and not me who'd moved first at the start.

'Why is this happening?' I kept asking. 'I just want my gold medal.'

Four hours after I'd crossed the line first, I was officially disqualified. I'd been riding an emotional rollercoaster, and it all came out when I fronted the media.

'I'm just numb right now,' I said as tears welled in my eyes.

'I didn't know anything was going on. I was told that I was in the clear. I was walking out to do my medal ceremony and they called us back and said there were still protests going on. No-one could tell me what it was about or who it was against.

'That's probably been the most disappointing thing because I still thought it was all right. I was getting told all these different stories and I was not ever once told the truth, never once told what was going on. I don't think that is fair. I am in this sport as a competitor and as an athlete just like anyone else. This is our career, this is our job. This is what we train for. To run the race, do the victory lap and then be told, "Oh no you can't have your medal now" is horrible. But I have to deal with it because that's just the way sport is.

'It didn't go my way and that's what I have to deal with, and I'm just going to use my emotions and my anger and my disappointment and put it into the hurdles and I hope I can come out on top.'

By the time I got on the bus to return to the athletes' village, I'd started to calm down. I'd proved I was the best runner on the night; I just didn't have anything to show for it. As I sat down next to Sharon and Eric, I looked up and saw the team management for England seated at the back of the bus. I gave them my best death stare, but then suddenly something clicked. This was going to be so awkward, and I felt we all needed to move on.

'I'm going to speak to them,' I told Eric.

'No you're not.'

'I am. I promise I won't be mean. I'll be nice, just shake hands and no hard feelings.'

Eric knew me too well, which was why he was petrified I would inflame the international incident further.

'You'd better promise me.'

I nodded and approached the English team manager. I tapped him on the shoulder, and his face dropped when he turned around.

'No hard feelings,' I said as I put out my hand. 'It's all good, don't worry about it.'

'Okay, thanks,' he said as we shook hands.

The following day I went to the track to chill out, and couldn't believe my timing as I arrived just before the 100m medal ceremony. As I watched the English girl receive the bronze medal and start playing up to the crowd, a man, who I was told later was the boss of UK Athletics, sat down next to me.

'I'm so sorry,' he said. 'I'm so embarrassed by the way our team handled that and how they protested against you. If it happened again I would never let it go through.'

I just shrugged my shoulders. I was over it. (Three days later, gold medallist Nigerian Oludamola Osayomi failed a drug test and was disqualified.)

The heat of the 100m hurdles was two days later, and I found myself more nervous than usual. While I was untroubled to progress in 13.02, it was a terrible race technically.

The bonus looking ahead to the final was that my training partner, New Zealand's Andrea Miller, had made it through after finishing third in my heat. Andrea had been with us on and off over the past year but had been forced to stay home in Australia because of a back problem. I hadn't seen her for three months until we got to Delhi, and was blown away with how good she looked. Clearly she'd worked hard while she was on the sidelines, and it had paid off.

It was great to have her in the race, as we got to warm up together, and Andrea was particularly excited as she was drawn in lane eight and I was in lane seven for the final. Given she'd started next to me so many times before, it was her comfort zone, and I found myself more nervous about her race than my own, as I wanted her to do well.

When we were behind the blocks I decided on an ultra-conservative approach to the start. There were going to be no mistakes, and I was happy to be the last one out.

I figured I had the speed and technique to make up the ground against the calibre of rivals I was up against.

I executed my plan perfectly. There were no issues with the start, and in normal terms it was an ordinary getaway, but I was quickly into my rhythm. By halfway I'd burnt off those close to me, with the only threat, Canada's Angela Whyte, down in lane four.

There was no way this gold medal was getting away from me, and I knew coming to the last hurdle it was mine. As soon as I cleared it, a massive smile broke out on my face. I could feel all the emotions I'd held in over the past couple of days start to come out as I crossed the line.

I'd won my first title in 12.67, with metres to spare from Whyte (12.98). I couldn't stop shaking my head with delight as I slowed down over the line. My euphoria went up a notch when Andrea grabbed me.

'What did you do?' I asked.

'I think I got a medal,' she said.

'No way!' I screamed as we both turned to look at the big screen. She was right. Andrea had won the bronze medal in 13.25. We both squealed and started dancing together.

I was so happy for her and momentarily forgot about my own achievement. We were going to celebrate in style together. It was going to be a big night, given Kieran and Mum had arrived in Delhi in time for the hurdles final.

The previous few months had been tough without my husband, and I was so happy that the two most important people in my life were there to share my first gold medal. I found them and had an emotional moment before Kieran gave me an Australian flag for my lap of honour. It was a good feeling to jog around knowing there was no way that title could get taken away.

I was so relieved. Twelve months previously, I'd almost retired. It had been a long haul to get back, and now I was the Commonwealth champion.

All I could think about was how big the party was going to be when I caught up with Sharon and Andrea afterwards. My coach had other ideas.

'You might want to have a think about that because they want you to do the 4x400m relay,' Sharon said.

'Noooooooooooooo.'

I'd planned to visit the Taj Mahal the next day, but that looked unlikely now. It turned out the relay team – who'd finished second in the heat behind India to qualify for the final – had had a meeting without me. They'd decided they wanted me on board and had sent Jody Henry out to find me.

I was petrified. I didn't want to let the girls down by not running, but I also thought I'd let them down by running. They wanted me to run the final leg in the team that included Henry, Pirrenee Steinert and Olivia Tauro. I knew I couldn't say no to running for Australia.

I didn't eat all day in the lead-up to the race. I despised 400s with a passion, and had never been so scared out on a track as I was waiting for my leg. By the time I got the baton off Olivia we were third, with a big gap to India and

England. I soon realised there was no way I was going to catch those girls.

The hard thing was that I didn't have anyone to sit behind, which would have helped give me an idea of how fast I should have been running. I got around the 300m bend and I could sense people catching me. The problem was I couldn't go any faster, and then the girl from Canada came around me on the bend and somehow hit me with her baton.

I'd gone from being caught in no-man's land to being now stuck on the inside and unable to get out. I was in a lot of pain over the final few metres as I desperately tried to catch her before staggering across the line in fourth place.

The lactic acid build-up was excruciating, and I immediately collapsed onto the track. I felt like I wanted to vomit. Jody grabbed me and lay me down, lifting my legs up to try to shake the lactic out.

All I wanted to do was crawl into a hole and die. They were going to bring a stretcher out, but I told them I'd be fine. However, when I tried to walk it felt like the ground was moving. I had to walk up three steps and I was so stiff that it looked like I was marching. Vomiting after training sessions was a regular thing for me, but I'd never experienced that much lactic acid.

I was eventually sick just outside the media area before making it to post-event control, where the Australian team doctor covered me in ice. I slumped in front of a fan. Twenty minutes later I was fixed. That's the one good thing about a lactic acid attack; when it passes, you're instantly back to normal.

Before I could get to the celebrating that had been postponed because of the relay madness, I had a message to pass on to my coach: 'Don't ever put me through that again.'

I was always favourite as a junior going into races … so being expected to win wasn't really daunting. It gave me confidence.

13

'If I'm going to win a gold medal at the Olympics, then I have to win the world championships.'

My declaration to Sharon came in our debrief session looking back at 2010. I then added: 'These two years are going to be the biggest of my life.'

My coach understood where I was coming from, but wanted to hedge her bets. 'I agree that if you are to win a gold medal in London, you have to medal at the world championships.'

'No. I have to win,' I repeated.

She seemed to get the message.

I wanted to be in the shape of my life for the 2011 world championships, which were being held in Daegu, South Korea, in August.

'I don't want to let anything stop me,' I said. 'I want to make sure I do everything I can to run fast and become the best.'

I'd already made one important decision about a key area: my diet. One of the things I could control was what went into my body, and this was highlighted to me by a fellow athlete. What started out as an innocent conversation over lunch ended up being a life-changing moment, and a potentially dangerous one.

I'd spoken about how I thought I needed to get a little bit leaner and maybe drop my skinfolds, but hadn't really looked into it.

'You can start by not eating those things, for a start,' she said, pointing to what I thought was a healthy chicken and salad sandwich.

By the end of the lunch I had a whole different outlook on food. I clearly had no idea about eating properly. Not that I ate badly by any stretch, but this was a whole new world. From that point on I was obsessed. Major carbohydrates such as pasta and bread – which were my two favourites – were out. Any little treats like chocolate or biscuits were gone, and I started measuring to the gram how much cereal I had each morning.

In my head I'd suddenly convinced myself that controlling my diet was going to win me the world championships. If I remained anal to the extreme, then I would win. If I didn't, I would lose. It was a scary mindset to have, which I was to find out later.

Another lifestyle change that was designed to keep my mind busy was a new job. I'd begun to think about life after the track and thought it would be good to have some qualifications behind me whenever that time came. I knew I could get a job at Mum's work any time, and I found a TAFE course for a traineeship in business administration, which I would be able to do at Bartercard. At the end of it I'd have a Certificate 3 in business administration, which sounded impressive enough. That was all well and good, but the problem was I had to understand how Bartercard operated, which was a lot harder than I'd figured.

Speaking of hard, I got to sit across from Mum at work – and she was one tough cookie on those phones! It's fair to say she didn't put up with much rubbish, and there were many times I was glad I wasn't the person on the other end of the phone.

Having a routine with work and training was a lot better than just lounging around on the couch in between sessions. I would do an early gym or pool session and be at Bartercard by 9.30 am, work until around 1.30 pm and then go to training at the track in the afternoon. Instead of sitting on my backside behind a desk the whole time, I raised my computer and keyboard so I'd be able to stand up and do my job. It might have been a small detail, but everything was geared towards Daegu in August.

On the track Sharon and I had again decided to limit my hurdling throughout the Australian domestic series because of my back. It worked for the most part until I got itchy feet after training had been going so well. A compromise was reached and we included the hurdles in my program at Perth and at the national championships. With virtually no training over the barriers, I still ran 12.85 in Perth, but my frustration with the 100m national record continued. My pursuit of Melinda Gainsford-Taylor's 11.12 again came up short. This time it was 11.20.

The national championships were in Melbourne on 15–17 April, and rather than focus on records – historically conditions were always bad for fast times at Olympic Park – we changed tack and I was chasing titles in three events: the 100m hurdles, 100m and 200m.

On the Friday I cruised through the heat of the 100m in 11.69 and then ran 11.51 in the semifinal. The following night I improved that again to claim my fifth national title in 11.38.

Four races in one day were on the menu for the Sunday, with heats and finals of the 100m hurdles and 200m. The hurdles was again solid, with victory coming in 12.83, while I enjoyed winning my first national 200m crown in 23.20. I found out afterwards that I was the first athlete in 43 years to win three national titles on the one weekend.

While we were keen to mimic a lot of 2010 in our preparation, there was one major difference – Kieran was coming with me.

We'd both struggled badly being away from each other for three months and agreed we couldn't go through that again. His business was up and running, but financially we could handle him being away. More importantly, for my sanity I needed him. His presence was going to make going back to Cologne bearable.

I'd come to the realisation that it was one of those places that was good to visit on holiday but not to stay in for too long. I found there was a combination of little things that conspired to wear you down. Not many of the locals spoke English, which did get to me after a while. The weather was always bad, and I couldn't even chill out in front of the TV because there was nothing that was watchable. Instead, I ended up spending hours stuck in the apartment looking at downloads of my favourite shows on the small screen of my computer.

What I also found myself looking at was my body in the mirror – all the time. Too much of the time. I kept looking to see if I was lean. In my mind I wasn't – what I was seeing was still the slightly chubby Sally from the previous year – but everyone kept telling me how fit I was looking.

It was weird.

I knew I had an issue, which scared me. But at the same time, the fact that I still wanted to eat gave me confidence that everything was still reasonably okay.

On the track I couldn't have been more confident with how I felt coming into my opening race in Lausanne on 30 June. It turned out to be a challenging evening, as we had to deal with a strong tailwind. For hurdlers it's actually harder to cope with that than a stiff headwind, because you have to try to keep yourself balanced.

Adding to the degree of difficulty was the fact that Danielle Carruthers was right on my tail the whole way, but I got the dip in on the line to win in 12.47 by .01 of a second. (The wind had been an illegal +3.3 metres per second.)

The American actually thought she'd won and started celebrating with the winner's flowers, which are presented at the finish line. I knew it was me, and Danielle was a touch embarrassed as she handed them back over. The bonus was I got to feel what it was like to run at that speed. While it was illegal, it was still the first time I'd broken 12.5, and knowing what it felt like was important for the future.

We weren't tapering for the competitions, with Sharon saying it was crucial that I continued to build fitness right up to the world championships. She had to plant these things in my mind ahead of time because I was always questioning everything.

'What I am doing this for?' I'd ask about why I was doing a speed endurance session the day before these big meets.

This added to our happiness about what I was producing on the Diamond League circuit, and we got a pleasant surprise in Birmingham. After winning the heat in 12.57, which was a meet record, two hours later we came out for the final in pouring rain. It wasn't exactly the backdrop I'd expected to produce another Australian record-breaking performance against, but my personal best was lowered to 12.48 – the fastest time in the world that year. Danielle

Carruthers had also run a personal best for second (12.52) while Virginia Crawford was third (12.79).

I decided the new record deserved a celebration, and a break from the 'rabbit food' that was all I'd been allowing myself to eat. Two slices of cheesecake were the prize, and I'd never tasted anything so good in my life. It was only a brief lapse, and the strict diet was back for our visit to Monaco, where once again the weather was hot and perfect for running fast.

The problem was I felt terrible in the lead-up and certainly wasn't expecting the 12.51 I clocked in claiming another victory. There was a new kid on the block chasing me, with American Kellie Wells grabbing second (12.58) and Tiffany Porter third (12.60). I got a lot of confidence out of running that fast while feeling absolutely crap. I knew that was a great sign looking ahead to Daegu in just over a month's time.

* * *

'Am I peaking too early?'

I was asking Sharon the same question over and over.

'No, Sal, these are the times you should have been running last year, but for a whole host of reasons it didn't happen.'

That seemed to make sense to me.

'So you're not surprised?'

'No, I'm not surprised.'

The final race before the world championships was in London at Crystal Palace, which was a track that historically was slower than the others. I was determined to keep my unbeaten streak going and felt good in the heat, winning it in 12.55. There were no mistakes in the final, which I won comfortably in 12.58 from Danielle Carruthers (12.67) and Tiffany Porter (12.78).

Now all everyone wanted to talk about was the pressure associated with going into a major championships as the raging favourite. I actually liked the position. While it's on a different scale, I was always favourite as a junior going into races, and got used to it, so being expected to win wasn't really daunting. It gave me confidence, as I knew these girls had to chase me. And they had a lot more work to do than I did.

I already knew I was in great shape. I was healthy, and they were the ones who had to pick up their game.

'You want to be the best in the world and that's what comes with it,' I told journalists after the race. 'I'd rather be running fast and have everyone talking about me than not running fast. I am conscious of [the added pressure], but that's what I want.'

We arrived in Daegu two weeks early, which turned out to be a masterstroke as it put me in an extra bubble of focus. It meant I could concentrate on exactly what I was there to do, and didn't have to stress about anything. I was in an apartment with a great bunch of girls, including Alana Boyd, who was my roommate, Dani Samuels and Hayley Butler.

The village was fun, but the food was shocking. There was a lot of outrage, but I didn't let it worry me. My attitude was that there was nothing you could really do about it, so you just had to find a way to deal with it.

Everything was tracking perfectly until I felt it go again. I was halfway through a hurdles session when my back tightened. I made the mistake of choosing to ignore it and pressed on. With each hurdle I felt the muscles getting tighter and tighter before it finally grabbed. Then I couldn't move.

It wasn't as bad as the 2009 episode, because I was able to get moving after a few seconds, so I wasn't totally freaking out. I went straight over to the physio and we were all confident that some rest and anti-inflammatory tablets would do the trick. As long as it didn't affect my program in the final week leading up to my first-round race, then I was able to remain calm.

After a few days off I went down to the small 150m track at the village for an activation session with the physio. He had me complete a series of drills to see how my back responded, and I knew Sharon was freaking out. She wasn't happy, but I went along with his directions. I survived that and was determined to stick with the program that had been mapped out months ago.

The following day I had a sprint session and it was terrible.

'This feels absolute crap,' I said to Sharon.

My calmness was starting to break.

'I'm running so slow. What I am doing today is not going to get me a gold medal at the world championships. What the hell is going on?'

And with that I stomped off and started to walk a lap.

I'd also asked Sharon what she thought the speed of my run-throughs equated to for the 100m. She estimated 11.5. That just made me even angrier, because an 11.5 pace wasn't going to win me a gold medal in the hurdles.

As I started the walk, Eric Hollingsworth approached and asked if he could join me. It was good to have someone other than Sharon to talk to about these things, and I wanted Eric's thoughts on what he'd just seen.

'Did you see that? It was just crap and slow,' I said.

He agreed, which was all I wanted to hear.

'Yeah, it was slow and I know what you mean that it's not going to get you a gold medal, but you know you are better than that,' Eric said. 'You know that at the world championships you're going to be.'

Before we'd left for overseas, I'd sat down with Sharon and had a heart-to-heart. While the odd blow-up was inevitable, we really needed to be on the same page.

'Can you please just hear me out sometimes,' I told my coach. 'I really need you to trust me as much as I trust you. It's really important because these are the two biggest years of my career, and I can't let anyone else disrupt it.

'We know what we've got to do to make me the best. Others don't understand – they haven't been with me for that long. They don't get it. They don't see me every day. They don't know what my body is like.'

This resolve was put to its greatest test in the final week leading into the first round of the 100m hurdles. I was scheduled to do a hurdles session out of the blocks, but as we walked to the track, Sharon suggested a change. At that stage I was unaware of her motives.

'I don't know whether hurdling is a good idea today,' she said.

'Why?'

'You've had a fair bit of treatment on your back and I think maybe it's too much to be hurdling today. Maybe we just do a warm-up stretch and then hurdle tomorrow.'

That meant I would be doing a hurdles session three days before I raced – the first round was on Friday, day seven of the championships – which normally wasn't what we did. I didn't like breaking routine ahead of big races and I suggested we make a decision after the warm-up and just see how I was feeling.

Sharon agreed, but unbeknown to me she was copping heat from team management. Eric and the medical team had effectively ordered Sharon not to let me go over the hurdles. He wanted me in cotton wool, as any sort of minor setback would end my championships.

After feeling good in the warm-up, I went and started setting up the blocks. Sharon just let me go as normal. The track was quite slippery and I needed someone to stand on the blocks.

'Hey Eric, can you stand on my blocks for me?'

He looked at me and then Sharon. 'Yeah, sure.'

I completed a couple of starts without issue and then Eric had to leave for a meeting.

My back had not been an issue, and as I was warming down, Sharon came over and told me about the blow-up. Just before he'd left, as I was at the other end of the track, Eric had walked past Sharon and said, 'This better not fucking lose her a gold medal.'

'No, it won't,' was Sharon's response.

I was so happy when my coach told me the story. Sharon had shown faith in me to know what my body was capable of doing in that session.

Instead of buckling under pressure and listening to the medical team, which she'd done in the past, she'd trusted me.

It was a pivotal moment in our relationship.

Everyone had started to take notice of me that year, with the unbeaten streak and the fact I was running super-fast.

14

'You're going to win then.'

Those were the words of Dani Samuels. We were sitting in our apartment and she was explaining how nervous she was about the week ahead. Dani had won the world discus title two years earlier in Berlin, but had struggled to deal with the pressure associated with the victory in recent times.

She was really feeling it now that the championships were upon us, and was having trouble sleeping. I remember in Berlin I had been the one who was still up at 1 am because I couldn't sleep, while Dani would be passed out at 10.30 pm. It had made me angry, because that was a sign of someone relaxed and confident going into a major championships.

Now the roles had been reversed. I was sleeping like a baby and Dani was climbing the walls. That was why she'd predicted my victory, and as soon as she said the words it also hit me – I was going to win.

There was one minor difference, though, that confused me. Dani was actually the one who was having dreams that she was going to win the world title again. I wasn't having any dreams, which for me was unusual.

After a miserable first couple of weeks in Daegu, the weather had turned for the better and was perfect by the time the championships began. The heats were in the morning and I was on song the moment I got to the warm-up track.

'This is the best warm-up I've done for a major competition,' I declared to Sharon.

'Yep, you looked amazing.'

As I went over each hurdle I was getting more and more surprised at how good I felt. Hayley Butler, who was a member of the 4x100m relay team, had been a hurdler as a junior and had come out to watch the warm-up.

'When you do your warm-up, every single person, as soon as you get onto your blocks, everyone stops and just watches you,' she said.

'Really? Thanks.' It was a nice little confidence boost just before I entered the competition arena.

While the warm-up had been outstanding, I was still concerned about the fact that I hadn't competed for three weeks. I had a history of not running well first up at a major championships after a break, and having that weird sensation of forgetting how to hurdle. Normally that resulted in a time of around 12.8, but I knew early in the heat that wasn't going to be the case this time.

Nevertheless I still wasn't expecting what appeared on the clock: 12.53.

'Wow,' I said out loud as I crossed the line. It was the fastest heat run in world championships history. I knew immediately what people would be saying. They would think I'd run the race of my life in the heat, that I'd gone too hard and would be dead for the next round.

Steve Hooker relayed a conversation he'd had with Irish hurdler Derval O'Rourke in a lift shortly after the first round.

'Did you see Sally?' he asked.

'She ran really fast, too fast for a heat,' O'Rourke said.

'No I reckon she looked pretty comfortable,' was my team captain's reply.

That was exactly how I felt, and I wasn't about to let a stupid curse mess with my mind. The 'Curse of the Cover' had become a major talking point in Daegu, given the unfortunate results for the athletes who'd featured on the cover of the daily program. Six out of the seven athletes who'd appeared on the cover, including Hooker, had bombed that evening.

The only successful one was actually a walker, so some people were saying that didn't count as it was off-site and not an event in the stadium.

I found out I was on the cover for day eight when I walked into the physio room and long-jumper Mitch Watt was there.

'Did you see the cover of the program?' Mitch said with this big cheesy smile on his face. 'You're on the front.'

It didn't bother me, but his excitement about it did.

'Why are you saying that with a big smile on your face, Mitch?'

He backtracked immediately. 'Oh, I didn't mean it like that.'

Apparently Sharon had been horrified when she found out and was telling people not to show me. She'd even tried to collect the programs around the apartment so I wouldn't see it.

'This is just a total sign of respect,' was Sharon's take on the curse. 'No-one else has made that cover that wasn't a defending world champion or a multiple world record holder. This is an amazing sign of respect, so just soak it up.'

The program was the last thing I was thinking about as I stood on the start line for the semifinal. I was in lane three, with my main danger, Dawn Harper, in lane five. My start was again brilliant and I felt so smooth over the hurdles. Everything seemed easy, and I cruised to victory over Harper. I knew it was good, but I was blown away when I saw the time: 12.36. It required a second and third look for it to sink in. I'd just taken .12 of a second off my personal best in the semifinal.

I looked up at Sharon in the stands and gestured my surprise by mouthing, 'What the?'

Everyone was screaming because they were as excited as I was about the time, which I was soon told was the equal fifth fastest time in history. It was also the fastest time seen in the 100m hurdles since Gail Devers ran 12.33 seconds in 2000, and would have won every Olympic title in history.

My disbelief soon turned to worry as I headed for the warm-up track, given I only had 90 minutes until the final. I was confused because I figured I must have run my legs off by clocking that time, but they actually felt good. Why wasn't I tired?

I started second-guessing myself.

'Have I just run too fast?' I asked Sharon as we walked a lap together. 'Are you sure I haven't run out of legs?'

Sharon was very calm.

'I've been waiting for this year for a very long time,' she said. 'You're going to run a lot faster.'

I couldn't comprehend that but I was intrigued. 'Well, what do you think I'll run?'

She didn't even blink. 'I reckon at least 12.30.'

I wandered off for another lap to mull over my coach's prediction. About halfway along I passed Usain Bolt, who was sitting down watching the big screen. The men's 200m final was on 20 minutes after my race.

'You're killing it,' he said.

I was completely caught off guard. Wow! Usain Bolt was talking to me.

'Thanks,' was all I managed, with a massive smile on my face.

Everyone had started to take notice of me that year, with the unbeaten streak and the fact I was running super fast. When I got back to Sharon, I asked her what she wanted me to do for the next hour.

'Nothing,' she said. 'I don't want you to do a thing. You've just run so fast you have to let your fast-twitch fibres settle down, so don't do anything. Just lie down.'

I was in good hands with Bruno, my favourite masseur, working on my legs. He was good value and always had a story to tell. After a bit of banter about nothing in particular, Sharon and I went for another walk. As we made our way around the track we watched my rivals going over hurdles, some even crashing into them.

'They're trying to find something,' Sharon said. 'You've just run 12.36. They're trying to find that extra thing that you've got.'

I liked her explanation. 'Cool,' I said.

With 20 minutes to go until I was required at the call room, I did some slow skipping and that was it.

I was ready.

* * *

'World record. Not today.'

I don't know where those words came from, but they suddenly came into my mind as I waited in the call room.

I'd never thought about the world record just minutes out from running a race before, which told me I must have been getting close.

'Surely not,' I said to myself as we walked out onto the track.

I was in lane three – sandwiched between two Canadians, Nikkita Holder and Phylicia George. My three American rivals – Danielle Carruthers, Kellie Wells and Dawn Harper – were all drawn out together on the far side.

After completing my run-throughs, I sat down on the lane box and took a deep breath. There was a calmness about everything.

As the camera came up close for the introductions, I smiled and waved.

I knew I just had to repeat what I'd been doing all year.

These girls can't go with me.

After getting settled into the blocks, I sat up, adjusted my hair and took one last look down the blue track.

Fast start. Strong start. Fast start. Strong start.

I nailed it.

Go. Go. Go.

I was in front over the first hurdle and travelling. My rhythm was perfect as I flowed over hurdles two, three and four.

I'm winning the world championships. Ahhhhhhhh!

I'd just gotten over the fifth hurdle and let out a muffled scream. In Beijing I'd realised I was leading over the fourth hurdle and got too excited.

Don't let it happen again. Stay focused.

I was clean over the next couple of hurdles and everything felt fast. I was moving.

Where are the others?

With two hurdles remaining I still couldn't see a leg out of the corner of my eye or sense the presence of anyone.

Keep running. Keep running.

The final hurdle was as smooth as the first.

I've done it. I'm the world champion.

I dipped for the line and then looked straight up at the clock: 12.28.

Holy shit. That's nearly a world record.

I screamed and kept running to where I saw a lot of people in yellow.

12.28. Have I really just run that fast?

My Australian teammates were going nuts in the stand as I bounced in front of them, screaming. An Aussie flag was thrown down, and as I put it around my shoulders, I saw Sharon making her way down the stairs.

We'd done it. We'd stuck strong and got our gold medal. She'd always said I was ready to run that fast and, as usual, she was right.

'Thank you. Thank you,' I said as she squeezed the life out of me.

I then took off on the most enjoyable lap of my life. There were Australian fans littered throughout the stadium, and my smile seemingly got bigger and bigger with every stride. I found Mum, Kieran and my manager, Robert, almost at the completion of my lap.

'I did it,' I screamed.

I was almost back to the finish line when David Culbert, a former Olympic long jump finalist and commentator from Australia, ran down the stairs and threw a program onto the track for me.

'Stuff the bloody curse,' I said as I stomped on it for the cameras.

I hadn't really comprehended what the time meant –
apart from the fact that I knew it was ridiculously fast –
until I got to the mixed zone and the interviews started.

My time of 12.28 was the fourth fastest in history. It
was a new world championships record, and the fastest
time run in the 100m hurdles for 19 years.

'I worked so hard to get here tonight,' I said. 'I haven't
missed a training session all year. I had faith in my coach
and my training.

'I've just given it all and finally come out tonight and
proved that when I want something badly enough, and I
stay focused enough, I can achieve it.

'I wanted it so badly.'

Many people were telling Sharon that my time was
the world record because there was a question mark over
Bulgaria's Yordanka Donkova, who ran 12.21 in 1988.
The three people in front of me in the record books had
competed during a period where drug cheats had dominated
the sport.

Maurie Plant was adamant. 'That was the world record
right there.'

I appreciated where they were coming from but my
response was simple: 'Well, it isn't.'

The medal ceremony wouldn't be until the following
evening after the 4x100m relay heats, in which I would be
anchoring the Australian team. There was still an official
press conference I had to do before I could get back to the
village to start celebrating.

ABOVE: Silver medallist Angela Whyte of Canada, me with the gold medal, and bronze medallist Andrea Miller of New Zealand on the podium for the women's 100m hurdles during the Delhi 2010 Commonwealth Games on 11 October 2010 in India. (Photo by Mark Dadswell/Getty Images)

BELOW: Racing over the finish line to become the world champion in the women's 100m hurdles at the 13th IAAF World Athletics Championships at Daegu Stadium on 3 September 2011 in South Korea. (Photo by Andy Lyons/Getty Images)

ABOVE: On the podium with my gold medal for the women's 100m hurdles at the 13th IAAF World Athletics Championships at Daegu, South Korea on 4 September 2011. (Photo by Mark Dadswell/Getty Images) BELOW: Usain Bolt (centre left) and I (centre right) were awarded male and female Athlete of the Year in 2011 at the IAAF World Gala on 12 November 2011 in Monte Carlo. We are flanked by the president of the IAAF, Lamine Diack, and Prince Albert II of Monaco. (Photo by Frederic Nebinger/Getty Images)

ABOVE: Leaping with excitement after winning gold at the women's 60m hurdles final at the 2012
IAAF World Indoor Athletics Championships in Istanbul, Turkey. (Photo by Gabriel Bouys/AFP/Getty Images)
BELOW: Winning the 100m hurdles at the IAAF Diamond League athletics meeting on 6 July 2012 in
Paris. (Photo by Ian Walton/Getty Images)

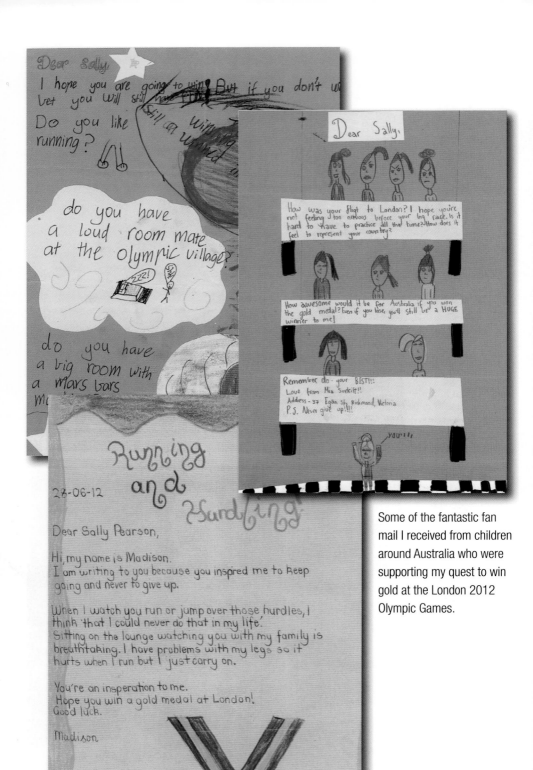

Some of the fantastic fan mail I received from children around Australia who were supporting my quest to win gold at the London 2012 Olympic Games.

ABOVE: Crossing the line to win gold in the women's 100m hurdles final at the London 2012 Olympic Games at Olympic Stadium on 7 August 2012 in England. (Photo by Ezra Shaw/Getty Images)

BELOW: The Omega photo finish image of the winning moment of the women's 100m hurdles final at the London 2012 Olympic Games. (Photo by Omega via Getty Images)

ABOVE: Hugging my coach, Sharon Hannan, after winning the gold medal in the women's 100m hurdles final at the London 2012 Olympic Games on 7 August 2012 in England. (Photo by Alexander Hassenstein/Getty Images)

BELOW: Dawn Harper of the United States kisses her silver medal, I hold up my gold medal and Kellie Wells of the United States holds her bronze medal on the podium at the London 2012 Olympic Games. (Photo by Quinn Rooney/Getty Images)

ABOVE: Drew Ginn, Kimberly Crow, me and Anna Meares during the Australian Olympic Team homecoming parade at Federation Square on 22 August 2012 in Melbourne. (Photo by Robert Prezioso/ Getty Images) BELOW: Racing against Tiffany Porter of Great Britain during the women's 100m hurdles at the IAAF Diamond League at Alexander Stadium in Birmingham, England in June 2013. (Photo by Matthew Lewis/Getty Images)

ABOVE: Winner Brianna Rollins and I, in second place, celebrate after the women's 100m hurdles final at the 2013 IAAF World Championships in Moscow on 17 August 2013. (Photo by Antonin Thuilliera/AFP/Getty Images)

LEFT: With my silver medal for the women's 100m hurdles at the IAAF World Athletics Championships in Moscow, August 2013. (Photo by Cameron Spencer/Getty Images)

While I was waiting to go into the pressroom, Usain Bolt arrived, as he'd just won the 200m.

'That was amazing,' he said.

Once again I was lost for words.

By the time I got back to the village it was well after midnight, and there was a note on my apartment door from Alana telling me to come up to Steve Hooker's room.

As soon as I opened the door, I was mobbed. My teammates were drunk and very excited with lots of group hugs, dancing and singing ensuing over the next couple of hours. Even though I was competing the next day, I still had a beer.

I figured I deserved it – I was the world champion.

'Don't worry, you're the world champion,' they all said, but I hated not ticking off one of my goals.

15

To get better you have to move on quickly.

That was the reality of the business. I'd learnt you had to find different goals straightaway to better yourself. There were two to tick off immediately after Daegu.

The first had been a long-term goal, and there was a $40,000 reason to have the second one on my list.

We were staying in Europe to chase the riches on offer in the Diamond League series, where the winner took home a healthy bonus. Given I had my eyes on another house on the Gold Coast, the extra 40k was going to come in very handy. The Diamond League final was in Brussels, but before that I had three races scheduled.

Six days after winning the world title, I was in Zurich lining up against the same girls. My Achilles had been sore in the lead-up and it had flared in unusual circumstances – on the dance floor. The celebrations for my world title had taken off after the 4x100m relay heats, even though they hadn't gone according to plan.

A stuff-up in the changeover from Melissa Breen to Charlotte van Veenendaal cost us dearly, and while I'd managed to catch the British runner in the final leg to finish third in the heat, it wasn't enough to qualify for the final.

I finally got my hands on the gold medal after the relay. The ceremony had been as good as I'd imagined – just the pure joy I felt watching the Australian flag rise above the stadium and singing along to the national anthem was simply magnificent.

We'd celebrated appropriately at a big party in the village. I'd had a few drinks but sweated all the alcohol out of my system by going crazy on the dance floor.

I woke up the next day with a sore Achilles, and by the time I got to Zurich it was a problem. Straightaway I sought American massage therapist Andy Miller, who was renowned on the tour as the best in the business.

His magic worked and by the morning of the race I was virtually pain free. That was positive, but I found myself feeling very nervous in the lead-up because I didn't want to lose the first time I ran with the title of world champion. My concerns were unwarranted and I ran surprisingly fast to win in 12.52, almost 3 metres ahead of Dawn Harper.

Next on the agenda was a trip to Rieti, Italy, which Sharon and I had been planning for months. For years I'd wanted to break Melinda Gainsford-Taylor's 17-year-old 100m flat national record of 11.12, and Rieti was the perfect setting. The Italian mountain town was at high altitude and the track was renowned for its fast times, with Asafa Powell setting the 100m world record there in 2007.

Everything seemed ideal; the only problem was I felt like crap at the start line and had a feeling no records were going to be broken.

I figured it was the jet lag, given it's always at its worst a week after you change time zones, but despite all of this I started well and at halfway was leading before Jamaica's Schillonie Calvert came over the top to win in 11.09.

I faded to finish second in the disappointing time of 11.24. Afterwards people couldn't understand why I was so upset at the result. 'Don't worry, you're the world champion,' they all said, but I hated not ticking off one of my goals.

It just made me even more determined to make sure I nailed down the second short-term goal. My next race was in Zagreb and I came away with my 19th consecutive win in the hurdles. Despite starting to feel the effects of a long season, I still managed to win in 12.68 with Harper second (12.81).

The scenario was simple for Brussels. I led the standings, but only by one point from American Danielle Carruthers, with Kellie Wells a further point behind – so it was a case of winner takes all.

I found myself feeling quite anxious leading into the race as I was going home the next day, so there was a lot of pressure to cap off the best season of my life on the right note. My start was once again on the money and I felt good over the first hurdle before something caught my eye.

The girl across from me in lane two was ahead. No-one had got near me out of the blocks that year and I was distracted by her in my vision.

What is she doing? Who the hell is this girl?

Suddenly I lost all awareness of what was happening.

Am I behind? Do I need to go faster?

The pace was hot going over the fourth hurdle, possibly too hot as I found out at the fifth. I hit it. Hard.

I stumbled and just managed to stay upright to get over the sixth, but then I was gone, hitting the deck after crashing through the seventh. I couldn't believe I'd fallen over and quickly got to my feet and walked off.

I was in shock and suddenly finding it hard to breathe. The tears were coming as Brigitte Foster-Hylton and Wells came over to see if I was all right.

'Don't worry, you didn't do it in the world champs final like I did,' said Wells, who was in medals calculation when she fell in Daegu.

Carruthers had won the final in 12.65 and the $40,000 bonus.

I was devastated. All I wanted to do was hide away and cry. It wasn't the money; I was just pissed off that I'd ended such an amazing year in that fashion. What made it worse was Sharon later had our biomechanist look at the race, and he said from the blocks to over the third hurdle I'd been on world-record pace.

That night Kieran copped the brunt of my tantrum, but eventually I calmed down enough to enjoy a couple of bottles of French champagne with my aunt and uncle, who'd made the trip to Brussels.

My arrival back home in Australia was going to be big on a number of fronts.

I was landing on the Gold Coast on 19 September, which was my 25th birthday, and my hometown was putting on a parade and civic reception to celebrate. Well, sort of.

The parade was happening, but it wasn't for my birthday – it was a welcome-home event that I was sharing with tennis player Samantha Stosur, who'd just won her first Grand Slam at the US Open. It turned out we'd both attended the same high school and had been members of the Queensland Academy of Sport.

I was surprised at the number of people who were there to see us presented with the keys to the City of the Gold Coast.

'I will be living the athlete's dream next year when I win the [London Olympics] gold medal,' I told the crowd, which was cheering loudly. 'Right now I've ticked one of two boxes, and that's winning the world championship.' It was a great occasion, but all I wanted to do was get home and reward myself by eating normally with a special treat of some chocolate and cake.

Two months later, I was back on a plane for a very good reason. I'd been nominated for the IAAF female athlete of the year and had to fly to Monaco for the awards ceremony. It was such an honour to even be considered, and I'd figured my fall in Brussels had probably cost me any chance of winning. Kieran and I were happy to just go and enjoy ourselves for a few days in one of my favourite cities.

That all changed when there was a knock on the door of our hotel room a few hours before the dinner. It was a woman from the IAAF, and she let herself in and sat down.

'I just wanted to tell you that you've won the award,' she said.

'What?' I almost screamed. 'Am I supposed to be hearing this?'

She went on to explain that they announced the winners to the international press before the dinner because the night went too late. I also had to attend a press conference with the male winner, Usain Bolt, in a couple of hours. It was a bit of a letdown to find out I'd won then, rather than hear my name read out on stage.

'It would be good if you could wear something smart to the press conference,' the lady said.

That was a problem. I'd only brought one dress with me, and I was in the most expensive place in the world. Luckily I knew of a place where Sharon had purchased something the year before, where the prices were half reasonable. We raced down there and found a simple black cocktail dress, which was perfect.

The best part of the press conference was the fact that I got to spend some time with Usain, which completely changed my perception of the fastest man on the planet. On TV he came across as cocky and sometimes disrespectful, but in real life he was the coolest guy ever and passionate about his running. We did a photo shoot together. His manager, who had his wife with him, was also there and we spent most of the time joking around taking our own photos.

Kieran and I had a couple of hours to kill before the dinner so we just chilled out up in our room. I left it until the last minute to get ready because the function was downstairs in our hotel, so we didn't have far to go.

Or so I thought.

When we arrived down there I saw a number of people in full military uniform and figured that Prince Albert of Monaco had invited some of his policemen to the event. A photographer took our photo and we sat down with a glass of champagne.

'I don't know anyone here,' I said to Kieran. 'Where are the other athletes?'

Everyone started to move into the dining room and I went over and looked at the seating plan.

'Kieran, our names aren't here. I can't see my name anywhere.'

Then I looked up at the sign. We were at the National Police Gala Dinner! I had the invitation in my bag and quickly pulled it out to find that the IAAF dinner was at the Sports Museum – not the hotel.

We bolted out of there. I was sprinting through the foyer of the hotel in this long, flowing gown when, thankfully, we spotted someone in an IAAF shirt.

'Where do we go?' I said.

He sensed our panic. 'Get in this car.'

We arrived at the function just as the IAAF president had started his speech and everyone was seated. Naturally, our table was at the very front. I was annoyed that the officials who'd been so keen to tell me I'd won earlier in the day hadn't bothered to ensure we had a ride to the dinner.

'We didn't know if you were coming!' one of them said.

What? I felt like jumping over the table at her. As if I wasn't going to attend – I was the goddamn winner!

The bonus was it meant I had some good material for my speech, and the crowd seemed to enjoy the tale.

We were then summoned to Prince Albert's table, where Kieran got to sit next to Usain and they talked about cars for half an hour.

While the night had been a crazy one, I found myself sneaking a few moments of reflection. When I was a teenager I'd watch the Golden League on TV and always wonder how you got to run in those events. What did you have to do? Did people tell you that you could go in those races? Did you ask someone if you could run in them? Did you need to have a manager? All these questions went through my mind as I was finding my way in the sport.

It's funny, because I'd always had the mentality that I wanted to be the best in the world. I never wanted to be the best in Australia; all my training and competing was aimed at becoming the best in the world. It was something that came naturally to me. Mum says I didn't get this drive from her and I figured this self-belief, which was a big reason for my success, had got stronger and stronger as I progressed in the sport. Believing in myself was the key to everything, and while this is always tested in younger athletes, those who can maintain it will always come out on top.

Even when I was running slow times, I was still thinking that was I going to be the best in the world.

Now I was.

* * *

It was the email I'd been waiting a long time to receive.

Part of being what I called a 'big deal' with my major sponsor, adidas, was having your name on your running spikes. It was a small thing, but to me it meant you'd made it. Only a select few adidas clients had their names on their running spikes, and it was seen as a privilege and honour to be given the opportunity. I'd actually been a little annoyed it hadn't happened earlier because some other Australian athletes, who were sponsored by ASICS, including Melissa Breen and 400m runner Sean Wroe, had their names on their shoes.

The norm was to go with a nickname. Olympic 400m champion Jeremy Wariner had 'Pookie' on his because it was his nickname at university. New 100m world champion Yohan Blake had 'The Beast' on his shoes. I didn't really have a nickname, but the closest thing we could think of was my email address – Kwikchik – which I'd set up years ago when I was starting out.

Even now I still get as excited as I did when I received my first package from adidas. Funnily enough, my first ever delivery from my sponsor went to the wrong house. I'd spent so much time looking over the catalogue and choosing what gear I wanted that I even wrote down the code numbers and included them in the email just to make sure they sent the right items.

We waited and waited for the package before finally I rang them up and asked what had happened. They said they'd sent it a month earlier, but it turned out someone had written down the wrong address. I tracked down where they'd sent the package and knocked on the door of the house where a little old lady answered and said she hadn't signed for it because it wasn't hers. Luckily the courier company still had it, so eventually they delivered my first bunch of goodies, which included the latest adidas T-shirts and tracksuits. There were similar excitement levels about the new spikes, which I was to pick up when I arrived in Europe.

I had no trouble getting back into training because I was still really focused on the two-year plan and knew only half the job had been done. We were going to stick as close as possible to the formula that had won the world title, but Sharon and I both agreed a change in the early part of 2012 was required. Given the lack of competition in Australia, a trip to Turkey in March for the World Indoor Championships was the challenge I needed.

My first race of the Olympic year was at the Brisbane Track Classic, and it showed I was tracking beautifully given I produced an 11.25 in the 100m. We deliberately programmed a busy racing season but didn't introduce the hurdles until Perth in February, where I clipped the sixth hurdle but still ran 12.86. A week later at the Sydney Track Classic there was significant improvement, with victory in 12.66.

The Olympic Games selection trials were on 2–3 March in Melbourne, where there was a change of scenery. A new track had been built in Albert Park after the state government had approved the knocking down of Olympic Park, which was being turned into a training ground for the Collingwood Football Club. It was sad to see a place where so many great athletes had competed gone, but there was some hope that the new facility would give more assistance to sprinters.

The weather was always an issue in Melbourne, but I was actually excited about the hurdles when I woke up on the morning of the race to find it raining heavily and the trees not moving outside my hotel room. Rain was better than wind, and the previous night I'd won the 100m in 11.67 but it was into a stiff headwind of −2.3 metres per second.

The damp but still conditions were ideal for the hurdles and I nailed it, clocking 12.49 – the fourth fastest time of my career.

'Holy crap!' was my reaction, and that's exactly what I told the waiting media pack.

'I know I can't swear, what can I say? It's really fantastic. It's really exciting, but at the same time I have to keep grounded and stay focused on the London Olympics; that's still a fair way away and a lot more training to go. I'm in good shape and loving it and I'm going to look after myself, that's all I can do.'

Shortly afterwards I was back on the blocks for the 200m. All I wanted was to break 23 seconds and I was convinced it would happen that night.

It didn't.

I fell just 3/100ths of a second short. The time of 23.02 equalled my personal best, which I'd set back in 2009. Why were the athletics gods punishing me?

My frustration was quickly forgotten as I boarded the plane for Istanbul the next day. I needed a hit of international racing again. I loved the craziness, the intensity, the vibe that you got at overseas meets – and without the world indoors, I would have been waiting until the middle of the year for my hit in Europe.

There was a small Australian team competing and there was an expectation that I would challenge the world 60m indoor hurdles record of 7.68. This was only my second time competing indoors so I was still a bit unsure about the whole thing.

My concerns were quickly erased in the heat when I broke the Australian record, clocking 7.85 to win easily.

The semifinal the following night was a different story. I learnt it wasn't a good idea to stuff up the start in a 60m race and I was forced to work super hard to get back into the race, which I managed to win in 7.93 from Belgium's Eline Berings (8.03).

There was a two-hour gap until the final, and while I was confident of victory, I felt I hadn't done enough to earn the world record because I wasn't experienced enough at the whole indoor caper. My hunch was right again, although I went very close.

I was a world champion again after crossing the line in 7.73 – the fourth fastest time in history – and just .05 off the world record.

Another goal had been ticked off the list. As I did a victory lap, my Australian teammate Henry Frayne was on the runway in the long jump. He told me later he was so pumped about my win that it helped him produce his best jump of the night to claim the silver medal.

I knew what was coming in the media conference afterwards, as I was aware of the growing theory that I was peaking too early in the Olympic year.

'Everyone thinks it every single year, and every year I have gone on and won … I don't know how many more times I have to prove I haven't peaked too early,' I said.

The medal ceremony was a bit of a fizzer, with the 'gold medal' more like a cheap plastic imitation.

I couldn't wait to get my hands on the real thing in five months' time.

I think I know how to keep myself grounded. I know how to stay focused and I know how to stay hungry.

16

'We hate you by the way, just to let you know.'
My training partner, Andrea, and I were letting Sharon know our thoughts ahead of what we knew was going to be a brutal training session. It was the session from hell, starting with a 300m time trial, followed by 3x250m sprints.

I only got through two of the sprints before I headed to the bathroom. It was so hot that I just went straight to the shower, still fully clothed, and vomited. I seriously felt like I was going to die.

Welcome to base training.

I wish you could go through the year without doing that sort of training and just be fast all the time, but that's not how it works.

One of the secrets to my success had been my appetite for training and unwillingness to take shortcuts. Sharon estimates I might have only missed a handful of sessions in our whole time together. I'd always enjoyed training, and even when I first started I showed I was willing to make sacrifices. While my friends were going out to parties at high school, I would stay home as I knew I had training the next morning. This was my own choice – no-one was forcing me to do it – but I'd been quick to realise that becoming the athlete I wanted to be required doing the hard yards.

I'd had two weeks off after the world indoors and had really let my hair down, particularly on the food front. Chocolate, ice-cream, raisin toast, peanut butter sandwiches … all the yummy stuff I was not normally allowed to touch was on the agenda. I made the most of it because I knew I wouldn't be doing it again until September.

The obsessiveness that had dominated my thinking regarding food the previous year was no longer a problem. I understood my approach had been dangerous, and I'd now found a healthy balance. I'd actually come to the realisation of how much of a problem it had become just before the world championships and had alerted Sharon to how I was feeling. While it hadn't affected my performance, it was a mindset that I knew wasn't sustainable in the long term, and I was glad I'd managed to work my way through it.

After two months of hard work, I was climbing the walls waiting for the calendar to click over to June so I could get on the plane to Europe. Everything had gone according to plan. I was fit and healthy, which had been the first box to tick. Now I had to transfer that to the racetrack.

That enthusiasm got zapped a little bit by the 29 hours of travel to Oslo for my first Diamond League race. I was pleasantly surprised with my heat run of 12.59, but the problem was the final wasn't for another 90 minutes.

By that stage the jet lag had kicked in, and I actually felt like passing out in the warm-up. My eyes were all red and I was questioning whether I was physically up for the task.

The start to the final was a mess. First Kristi Castlin took forever to get ready on the blocks and then put her hand up just as we were about to go. Then heptathlete Jessica Ennis false-started, which delayed it again and got me more and more frustrated.

When the field finally got away, I didn't feel that great throughout the race and was happy to get the win, but I wasn't expecting the time – 12.49. How the hell did I do that? I looked up into the stand at my agent and shook my head.

I'd been nervous about my opening race, and it was good to send a message to the rest of the girls, reminding them who was the boss. Castlin had finished second in 12.56 with Tiffany Porter third (12.70).

As I cooled down, though, my back started to stiffen noticeably. The plane trip and then two races straightaway wasn't ideal. My next race wasn't for two weeks, which gave me plenty of time to get my bearings and, more importantly, to manage my body.

My next race was at a low-key meet in Nivelles, a small village in the middle of Belgium, and a number of my Australian teammates were also competing there. In the 100m I was matched against Melissa Breen and I was very happy with the race, which I won in 11.20 – my fastest time for more than a year. There wasn't much competition in the hurdles, which was why I was pleasantly surprised with my winning time of 12.52.

The stakes went up a notch for my next outing, which was at the stadium where it had all started for me nine years earlier. Back then I was a teenage relay runner; now as I lined up for the Diamond League meet in Paris I was the reigning world champion and the fastest hurdler in the world.

The excitement of being back at one of my favourite tracks had the adrenalin pumping. It was channelled in the right direction as I started brilliantly and, despite clipping a hurdle mid-race, kept my unbeaten run going. As I crossed the line I instantly looked at the clock and then screamed in delight. I'd just run 12.40 – the third fastest time of my career.

I grabbed the winner's flowers from the official just a few metres past the finish line while still in stride and kept going straight to the crowd, where I flung them up into the stand. How good was that?

I was bouncing around on the track because I couldn't control my excitement. I'd won easily from Virginia Crawford (12.59) and Tiffany Porter (12.74). And I'd done it while clipping a hurdle. Imagine if I hadn't? Then that was a 12.3 race.

With a month to go until the Olympic Games, I was at the top of my game.

* * *

I didn't want to be there.

The Croydon Park Hotel had never been a favourite. It was where we stayed each year for the London Grand Prix because it was near the Crystal Palace track. But the hotel was old and loud, to the point where you could hear everything that was going on in the rooms next to you.

I was already a bit anxious about my final race before the Games because my back had been really stiff in the days after Paris. The conditions when we got to the track didn't help my mindset, given rain was falling and it was mayhem at the warm-up track. There was a wheelchair race on before the opening round of the hurdles, so two lanes of the track were cordoned off for them, which left four lanes for 16 hurdlers to warm up.

It was a disaster.

Sharon was putting some hurdles out for me, but there were people in the way. Then I wasn't happy with the hurdles' position and was trying to move them, so we were both getting cranky at each other. In the end I warmed up over three hurdles instead of the normal four, and then when I got out to the track I was still a bit distracted as I set up my blocks.

Then without really realising it, I broke my routine. Normally I'd practise a start out of the blocks and just go three or four steps before stopping and coming back. I'd then repeat the process, but rather than stop, I'd continue on and go over one hurdle. It was what I'd done hundreds of times.

Not this time.

Instead of pulling up after four steps, I continued on and went at the hurdle. The problem was I didn't have the speed I normally would have, and as a result my lead leg went under the hurdle. In what almost felt like slow motion, my body flipped over the hurdle and I fell head-first onto the track. I managed to get my hands down first and then slid all the way down, almost coming to a rest underneath the second hurdle.

What the hell just happened?

'Woooooooaaahhhhhhh,' I heard the crowd go up.

I was so embarrassed and quickly got to my feet. An official walked over to see if I was all right. 'Calm down and take a deep breath,' he said.

I just wanted to get back to the blocks and do another start. I quickly checked them and then took off at a million miles an hour. There were no problems this time as I sailed over the first and then a couple more just to make sure there were no issues.

But as the starter called us up for the start, I could feel that my back – which had been an issue the whole time I'd been in Europe – hadn't appreciated my little accident.

Kellie Wells was in my heat and we were alongside each other the whole way before I managed to get the dip in first to win in 12.53, just .01 of a second ahead of the American.

I quickly made my way back out to the warm-up track because I knew I was going to need some treatment. For the first time I had my own physio, Britt, in attendance, which was fortuitous for us. She had some work to do as I had sore spots on my butt, glutes and back.

We had 90 minutes until the final so there was plenty of time to work on the problem areas. I was constantly up and down from the treatment table. I'd do one run through and then come back for more work as we tried to loosen up my back. It wasn't the ideal preparation for a key race, but physically I had the all clear to go – although, mentally, I was struggling. I just wanted this day to end. The quicker I got out of Crystal Palace the better.

Apart from the tightness in my back I wasn't sensing any mental demons from the earlier fall at the start and I got away with my customary speed over the first hurdle in the final. At halfway I was in front and seemed to be holding it together, but then I sensed something was off. It felt like I was running with flat feet. I sensed Wells come at me over the last two hurdles, but there was nothing there. As we crossed the line I knew I'd stuffed it up. The American had won in 12.57, just .02 of a second ahead of me.

My mood darkened even further as I watched Wells's reaction to the victory. She'd broken out into some sort of dance routine and was hamming it up to the crowd.

I was in no mood for talking and stormed through the mixed zone without comment.

'What the hell was that?' were my first words to Sharon as my emotions started to boil over. While I was disappointed to have lost my final race in the lead-up to the Games, what was pissing me off more was how technically poor I'd been. I had no explanation for it. My back was a little stiff, but I wasn't using that as an excuse.

What scared me was the Olympic Games were only three weeks away, and if I served that up again I could kiss any chance of a medal goodbye, let alone one with gold on it.

'Let's just put it down to a bad day,' Sharon said.

Eventually when the anger subsided and the tears went away, I agreed with my coach. There was no use stewing on it, and the next day we found the perfect distraction.

Kieran and I had been based at my aunt's house in Kent, just 25 minutes away from Tonbridge, which was where the Australian team was going to be based in the lead-up to the Games. We'd been travelling there each day for training, as the facilities at the prestigious Tonbridge School were first-class.

They'd been so welcoming and had gone out of their way to help us, even marking special lines for my hurdles on the high jump runway because we wanted to train with the crosswind at my back.

This was all part of Sharon's master plan to break the world record. We'd visited Tonbridge 12 months earlier to have a look around and my coach had investigated the wind. The locals told her that it was consistently strong coming down through the valley and seemed to always blow across the track.

That's why we trained along the high jump area and not the normal track – because Sharon wanted me to get my legs used to turning over super fast. The wind pushing me along made sure that happened, and with each training session I'd become more and more comfortable. Her theory was that if you trained your mind and body to move at extreme speed, then when it happened in an Olympic final you'd be able to remain in control.

Being around my family and in an English-speaking country with familiar food and television was a welcome change, and we loved it.

For a distraction we made a visit to Thorpe Park, a theme park in nearby Surrey. There was a big group of us – my aunt, her four children, two of my cousins and their friends – and it was so much fun. The rides and games certainly helped take my mind off hurdles and dancing Americans for a few hours.

As a precaution we took it easy with training over the next few days, as our greatest fear was my back flaring again. I was still struggling to get my head around the Crystal Palace debacle, but that all changed when I saw the results of Wells's next race. She'd competed in Lucerne,

Switzerland, three days later and had finished third in 12.79.

Suddenly, it all made sense: Wells had been at her absolutely best in London while I'd had a bad day.

'If they can only just beat me by two hundredths of a second on a bad day, they haven't got a chance at the Olympics,' I told Sharon.

What had been forgotten in the fall-out from my last race was that a week earlier I'd run 12.40 in Paris. That was a clearer indication of where I was at and, more importantly, I knew the others weren't near it.

* * *

'I'm the hunted.'

I was sitting on a stool in front of the world's media at the Adidas Centre for my final press conference. The track and field program at the Games started the following day, and everyone wanted to know how the gold medal favourite was handling the pressure.

'Everyone is chasing me,' I said. 'But at the same time it keeps me on my toes and I love to go out and race. I love competition; that's what I thrive on. If it all goes to plan I should be winning, especially with my personal best as it's much faster than everyone else in the race so they have a lot of catching up to do if they are running at their best.

'I have been competing for Australia since I was 16 years old. I've been to an Olympics; I've been to four world championships now and two Commonwealth Games. I think I know how to keep myself grounded. I know how to stay focused and I know how to stay hungry.'

A question I got asked all the time was: How do you control your nerves? People understandably saw competing at an Olympic Games as a scary experience because of the pressure and expectation you had to deal with. I tried to spin it around to a positive. The key thing for me was I'd raced over the hurdles a million times before and, while it's obviously different because it's an Olympic Games final, that's just a title. It's still a 100m hurdles race against girls who I'd run against every single time in Europe over the previous couple of months.

I'm lucky in a sense because I have so much fun out there on the track that I haven't had to work on that side of my mentality. Running the actual race is really exciting for me. The tough time is getting ready for the race, when that nervous energy hits and you're feeling sick in the stomach. That's when I ask myself: 'Why the hell do I do this? Why do I enjoy this?' But then, the moment I cross the line, I'm always like: 'Wow, how much fun was that?'

My final training session was after the press conference, because the first round of the 100m hurdles was four days away.

I had some new Olympic shoes to try out and they looked amazing, with a faint Australian flag on them. My nickname was now on the inside and I chuckled when on closer inspection I realised there was a spelling mistake – it read 'KWICKCHICK' rather than 'KWIKCHIK'.

I was already battling my superstitions about the shoes anyway. Adidas, who'd stuck by me since 2005, wanted me to wear my normal shoes in the heats and then the special Olympic ones in the semifinal and final. Given how much they'd done for me over the journey, I didn't want to let them down, but as a rule I preferred to wear the same shoes for the whole competition.

I could sense the anxiety building over the situation but I was proud of myself for not letting it take over.

'Sally, you're not going to get a silver medal because you're wearing different shoes,' I kept telling myself. 'It's okay; it's not going to make any difference.'

This fight in my head was over fairly quick and I didn't give it another thought after that.

Sharon liked to do a ten-day taper, which involved doing absolutely nothing for the final three days. That drove me insane because I felt like I hadn't done enough and should be out there doing something. The idea was that on race day I'd be so excited and have all this energy to burn because I hadn't trained for three days. It was like I'd been caged up and then finally let loose.

That year, I'd finally gotten to experience an Olympic Games Opening Ceremony. We'd been brought in by bus from Tonbridge for the night, which turned out to be as good as I'd imagined. It started off a bit weird, though, because when we walked into the stadium it was in darkness and the only lights were the small ones they had on the seats. From the track you couldn't see behind them to make out if there were people there, and initially I thought the place was virtually empty. I could make out a few figures in the stands but I was like, 'Oh my God, this is really embarrassing for the organisers.'

I couldn't have been more wrong.

When the lights went on I realised the place was packed, and it looked incredible. There was a lot of noise and it was a goosebumps moment. I was loving every second of it until about halfway through, when I realised I was busting to go to the toilet. It got to the point where I couldn't even take in the lighting of the Olympic flame because I was sitting down, crunched over and praying that there was a toilet nearby. I was seriously in pain. When the ceremony finally finished, I couldn't even run to the toilet; instead it was a slow walk outside the stadium before we found any type of toilet.

We'd eventually made it into the athletes' village a couple of days before the start of the athletics program because there was a shortage of space, so we had to wait until some of the competitors – mostly the swimmers – who were on early in the Games had finished and could be moved out. But village life was again great and it was almost like I got into this Olympic daze where I just went with the flow and, before I realised it, it was race day.

I was rooming with Alana Boyd, and we had the normal crew in our apartment area, with Dani Samuels and javelin thrower Kim Mickle in the room next to us. Pole vaulter Liz Parnov and the other javelin thrower, Kathryn Mitchell, shared a room, while 400m hurdler Lauren Boden and Melissa Breen were across the hall. They were all pretty easy girls to get along with, but we hardly saw each other because everyone had different training times and we also respected each other's space.

The bonus was we had live streaming of events on the TV in our rooms, so I got to watch a lot of other sports, in particular gymnastics.

I like to go to the stadium once before I compete, so I went out for the first night of the athletics with Kim Mickle, as Melissa was running in the heats of the 100m, and Dani was also in the discus qualifying.

There had already been a lot of talk about the track, which had been dubbed the 'Magic Carpet'. This came about after hometown hero Jessica Ennis had produced an incredible time in the 100m hurdles, which had been the first event of the heptathlon on the opening morning. She'd run 12.54, which was a world record for the event in the heptathlon and was the same time Dawn Harper had run to win gold in the Beijing Olympics.

Sharon was particularly pleased as she backed my technique to handle a super fast pace compared with my rivals. Hurdlers can get in trouble if the track is faster than normal and the speed is at a level they aren't accustomed to, which generally leads to mistakes. What it told me was that I had to get my arse into gear.

I was a really bad watcher. I hated how you weren't in control of anything when you were seated in the stands. Dani was really nervous because she'd been struggling, and we were all praying that she found one big throw to get her into the final. Thankfully she did, and we were screaming and carrying on, which got a thumbs up from her.

The noise in the stadium, particularly when Ennis did something, was what stuck in my mind from my reconnaissance mission. Unfortunately, I wasn't thinking about the noise – I wish I had been – when I entered the stadium three days later for the heats of the 100m hurdles.

Without any warning, my back had gone again. I had no idea where it had come from, but I was in pain as I tried to do some run-throughs at the warm-up track. After every rep I'd have to go back to the physio for a quick manipulation of the spine, wait 20 seconds, and then go out and do another rep.

In the call room I normally liked to move around a bit just to keep the legs warm. Everyone else was doing it and I tried to go for a 5-metre skip but couldn't do it. I just had to sit there, as there was nothing I could do about it. While I was in pain, it wasn't going to stop me, and I knew I was in good shape, so it was just a matter of getting across the finish line.

My warm-up in the stadium was one run-through over the hurdles and that was it, because the back was hurting too much. I figured that once I got down in the blocks adrenalin would take over.

Despite the discomfort, I still had in my mind that I wanted to mimic what had happened at the world championships the previous year. That meant I wanted to run the fastest heat of the morning. I'd noticed Kellie Wells had won an earlier heat in 12.69 and I knew I'd run 12.53 in Daegu, so there were some figures in my head.

Thankfully I'd been right about the adrenalin, because once the gun sounded my mind was clear. While I didn't hurdle great, I cruised home in 12.57 without trouble, which at least brought a smile to my face.

Lolo Jones won the final heat in 12.68, but she wasn't who I was worried about. Jamaica's Brigitte Foster-Hylton, who'd had the second fastest time for the year coming into the Games, had stumbled midway through the race and was out of the Games.

I was in the middle of a TV interview when I saw her rush past me in tears. I broke away from the interview mid-sentence and went over to comfort her, because it was heartbreaking to see that happen to anyone.

Getting through the mixed zone was the next task, with everyone keen for a quick word. What I found out during my way through was that my time had been the quickest heat run in Olympic history.

Back at the warm-up track I jumped straight into an ice bath, and despite the back problem, I was quite calm. I was determined not to stress out about it. I'd learnt my lesson from 2009, when I'd got that worked up before the race because of my injury that I'd wasted all my energy.

There was a composed feel about the rest of the day. I went back to the village, had some lunch and more physio work before just chilling out and watching some other sports on the TV. Sleep came easily, and after eight hours I woke with a smile because the date I'd had burned into my head for a couple of years – Tuesday 7 August 2012 – had finally arrived.

When you stop
and think about
what a small space
of time that is,
that determines
extreme euphoria
or heartbreak, it's
scary.

17

I t was always the walk that did it.

The walk from the village to the stadium bus was when I mentally flicked the switch. I was now in my zone, and there would be no distractions. I'd managed to keep relatively chilled out during the day, and it was only when I'd had a shower and started to get my numbers and gear ready that the nerves hit.

I was in the second semifinal at 7.23 pm, with the 100m hurdles final at 9 pm.

The good news was my back was nowhere near as bad as the previous day and I was able to warm up properly. I found that music helped take me to a relaxed place while I bounced around the track. It was an escape from the seriousness of what I was about to do. As soon as I took the headphones off I was always taken a bit by surprise. 'How quiet is it?' I asked.

Everything had gone well until we got to the call room. Dawn Harper was in the semifinal ahead of me, so I was anxious to see what time she ran. I wanted to be the fastest qualifier for the final because I felt it reminded the others that I was still the one to beat.

As soon as Harper's results flashed up, I was momentarily stunned. And then angry. She'd won in a personal best time of 12.46.

'Jesus,' I said.

How could she run that fast? She'd never done that before in a semifinal. I had to respond and clearly work a lot harder than I'd planned. As we gathered at the blocks I was more fired up than I'd been in a while. I had to beat her time. I had to.

It was almost the perfect start and I was clearly a long way ahead by the first hurdle. There was no relenting, although again I clipped the eighth hurdle, which was exactly what I'd done in the heat. It was only a momentary glitch and I knew the race was fast as I cleared the last and started my dip for the line.

'Yeeessssssss,' I yelled as I crossed the line and pumped my fist when I saw 12.39 on the clock.

I'd done it, and almost straightaway I started to do my calculations comparing the time with the world championships – it was .03 of a second slower than Daegu.

For some reason, right then I knew I wouldn't be breaking the world record in the final. But what made me not dwell on that thought was the next thing that entered my head: I was going to win the Olympic gold medal. I just had to make sure I kept it together over the next 90 minutes.

When I met Sharon I was having a bit of trouble with my breathing because I was still so hyped from the semifinal run. Finalists were offered a buggy to take them back to the warm-up track, but we decided to walk because I needed to calm down and slow my breathing down. It worked, and when we got there Sharon suggested we just stroll a couple of laps.

'I have to win this race. I can't lose this Olympic final,' I said.

'You won't. You won't,' Sharon kept saying.

I didn't stop. I don't know if I was telling her or I was telling myself.

'I can't lose this Olympic final. I can't let them win it. I have to win it.'

My coach was emphatic. 'You will.'

After some light exercises it was time. Sharon walked me to the call room and we talked about the eighth hurdle.

'You have the feel of the track now, so going into hurdle eight you just have to chop your stride,' she said.

'Yep, I can do that.'

Then we stopped and embraced.

'It's your night to shine, Sal,' Sharon said. 'All of the flashes are going to be for you. Go out and do it.'

* * *

The wait was annoying.

For the heat and semifinal we'd been rushed through the call room, but it was the opposite for the final. My nerves were increasing by the minute. I didn't like sitting for long periods because if I did, I knew my back would stiffen.

When we finally got out onto the track I was feeling good and focused. But again there was a delay. This time there was a medal ceremony that held us up, and as we were waiting it started to rain, which made me chuckle. Of course it was going to rain on my night; we were in England, which has the worst weather, so it shouldn't be a great surprise.

I just wanted the race to start – but now they had to do the introductions, which always took forever. Each runner was introduced with their name, country and achievements. I was in lane seven, so it seemed like ages before the cameraman was in my face. I knew I'd get a good reception because it had come out in the lead-up to the Games that because my mother was a local there was a possibility that I could get an English passport.

The British journalists had jumped on it and kept asking me if I would consider swapping allegiances. That was never going to happen, but the crowd had clearly embraced me as I got a massive cheer, which was a nice shot of confidence.

Once the starter called us up, I started working my way through my starting cues.

Fast start. Strong start.

My heart was racing, but then I realised they also had mega-loud heartbeats echoing through the loudspeakers in the stadium.

You've got to be kidding me.

They left them beating right up until the starter called 'Set' and then switched them off.

Fast start. Strong start.

It felt normal. It wasn't anything out of the ordinary, but I was safely out and over the first hurdle.

Keep it together.

My rhythm was good as I approached halfway.

What happened in the next six seconds changed my life forever.

When you stop and think about what a small space of time that is, that determines extreme euphoria or heartbreak, it's scary. Sit down and literally count to six. It blows my mind every time.

I wasn't counting midway through the Olympic final, but my mind was racing as I pleaded with myself to stay upright. Then I pleaded with the athletic gods to ensure I had crossed the line first and not Dawn Harper.

Now everything was slow. It had gone from one extreme to the other. Frantic thoughts and movement in the race to standing still, staring at a screen with the future direction of my life depending on what appeared on it.

I'm not a religious person, but praying was the only thing I could do. I thought I'd won; I just needed confirmation. Then it appeared. My name. First.

I screamed and fell to the track. I was on my hands and knees, gripped by shock.

I'd beaten Harper by .02 of a second. American Kellie Wells came up and grabbed me in a massive bear hug because she'd won the bronze medal in a personal best 12.48. Lolo Jones had again missed out, finishing fourth in 12.58.

'Where's Sharon?' I started screaming.

I saw the Australian team was just past the finish line and I located Eric Hollingsworth, who was on a chair jumping around.

'Where's Sharon?'

He was looking at me and pointing to his right, but I was confused as I was only looking at him and not his hand. My brain was frazzled – I'd just won an Olympic gold medal.

Then I spotted her and she made her way down to the front where we hugged like never before.

'Thank you so much,' I kept saying. 'Thank you.'

I could tell she was excited, but the overwhelming feeling for both of us was relief. It had been a two-year build-up, and the pressure had been intense – but we'd done it.

In reality that dream had started 12 years before, when I saw Cathy Freeman win in Sydney. Now, I was also an Olympic champion! And I'd set a new Olympic record in the process.

The victory lap, with Aussie flag draped around me, went way too fast. You're on such a high that you can't help but go faster than normal, and I felt like I could even run a 50-second 400m.

At the 300m mark I saw my aunt with her friends, which set off more screaming. I had no idea where anyone else was and I was too busy soaking up the well wishes from the crowd, which was giving me a standing ovation.

Then I spotted Mum, Kieran and Robert just up from the 100m start. Seeing the looks on their faces pulled at the heartstrings. It was a magical moment.

I learnt later that they'd almost had a disaster with the tickets. Their original tickets had been really bad seats, so Robert had arranged with adidas to swap for some better ones. But then on the train ride to the stadium at 5pm, Kieran had noticed the tickets they'd been given were for the morning session. A few frantic phone calls later and everything was thankfully sorted.

I felt like I was floating as I made my way to the mixed zone.

'I don't feel anything right now,' I told one of the television interviewers. 'I've just wanted it for so long.'

It took me 40 minutes to slowly snake my way through the press before the three medallists were taken into a press conference. That was a lot of fun because I got on really well with Kellie and Dawn, who was like a comedian a lot of the time.

The medal ceremony wasn't until the next night, which was very frustrating.

I had more TV commitments and received a nice surprise when I bumped into my good friend Australian cyclist Anna Meares on my way back to the village. I hadn't even known she'd been competing that night, let alone that she'd also won a gold medal, until I was in the mixed zone after my race and people were asking me what I thought about Anna.

Everyone had decided to shield the result from me because they didn't want to put extra pressure on me. There was more screaming and hugging with Anna before I finally made it back to my apartment at 3.30 am.

There was no-one there and all the lights were off, so I sat on my bed and got my computer out. I'd switched off Facebook for the last few days because I didn't want it to be a distraction. It was nice to go through all the messages, but my peace only lasted ten minutes before Alana and Dani walked in and the celebrations began again.

After a couple of hours' sleep, I was up and back in the media circus, starting with a joint press conference with Anna, which was lots of fun.

I finally got to spend some quality time with Mum, Kieran and Robert at a Qantas cocktail party before heading back out to the stadium to get my hands on that gold medal. It was a joke that Kieran and Mum had to again pay for tickets – we're talking several hundred pounds – just to be out there to see such an important moment in my life.

The medallists were told to be there an hour beforehand, and when we arrived they said there would be a 20-minute delay. That soon turned into an hour. The three of us were soon sick of being stuck in the medal ceremony room, so we decided to go outside and watch some athletics.

When we got up to the athletes' stand, the gates were shut because the area was full.

'Are you serious?' Kellie Wells said. Her boyfriend, Netherlands sprinter Churandy Martina, was about to run, and she was screaming at the attendant to let us in.

It worked, and we sat there for a while before heading back to the medal ceremony room, where again we were told there was a delay.

Luckily Kevan Gosper, the Australian representative from the International Olympic Committee who was presenting the medals, was there and he offered to take me up to the royal box. I felt like the queen sitting up there in the front row, and I texted Kieran, who looked up and saw me doing my best royal wave.

It turned out they'd delayed the medal ceremony because the women's long jump was getting exciting, which pissed me off because the hurdles final the previous night had been delayed because of a medal ceremony.

By the time we got out to the medal dais, the stadium was half empty and it felt like a bit of an anti-climax. It was disappointing, and I wasn't feeling the way I should have been until they started announcing Kellie's bronze and for some reason I felt tears welling. I kept them away, and they were well and truly gone by the time the gold medal was being placed around my neck.

Touching the gold medal instantly made everything real.

The sound of the Australian national anthem being played throughout the Olympic stadium also brought goosebumps.

I had a permanent smile on my face for the next few days as I soaked up my new title of Olympic champion.

It was only when I went back to the track a couple of days later that it disappeared. I was planning to continue racing in Europe because I was desperate to claim the Diamond League title that had eluded me the previous year.

But halfway through my first drill, I knew that wasn't going to happen. My back was hurting again and I couldn't do anything.

'I think I'm going to have to pull out of the rest of the season,' I told Sharon.

Then I burst into tears.

'Why am I crying? I'm the Olympic champion,' I sobbed.

We decided to delay announcing my decision because I didn't want to go home on the charter flight with the rest of the Australian team. I wanted to spend some more time in England with my family, as my aunt had a special gold party planned.

She went above and beyond. In just three days, she transformed her house into gold. There were gold posters and ribbon from floor to ceiling in every room. Each guest had to wear gold, and they were presented with a Cadbury's chocolate gold medal when they walked in the door.

My grandfather had died just before I won the IAAF Athlete of the Year, and Mum's sister, Wendy, kept his ashes above the oven in the kitchen.

To mark the occasion, she added some little gold flakes into the urn. 'Look, Michael is here too,' she said.

It was the party to end all parties, and a perfect way to celebrate what had been a perfect year.

The key to optimal performance in training and competition is motivation and now it was back …

18

Serena Williams was being interviewed on TV at the Brisbane International when my ears pricked up at one of her answers. The best female tennis player in the world had been asked about how she backed up after such a successful 2012, when she'd won two grand slams and gold at the Olympic Games.

'You just have to say that you didn't do well to yourself, that it wasn't good enough,' Williams said. 'That's how you keep going.'

It was so true. There was another quote I'd also recently heard from Rafael Nadal's coach – his uncle Tony – about keeping him motivated.

'You have to keep them hungry, you have got to keep them wanting more.'

I wanted more.

I was only 26 and there were more world championships to win, more Commonwealth Games gold medals to win. And of course there was an Olympic title to defend in Rio in 2016.

It was a crazy ride when I got home from the Olympics. There'd been an endless number of dinners and functions to attend, and for the first couple of months the longest Kieran and I spent at home in one block was three days.

We did manage to escape to New Zealand for ten days to go snowboarding, which was one of those things I wasn't normally allowed to do.

I returned to training on 15 October. We'd thought the long break was the right thing to do for my back, but in fact it seemed to exacerbate the problem. It was stiff and tight when I started moving again on the track, and we decided then that there would be no hurdling in the domestic season.

Scans of my back revealed I had a degenerative disc, which I was going to have to manage for the rest of my career.

I soon realised I was biting off too much by training and also travelling around the country with my gold medal. By November I was actually getting quite stressed, as my back was hurting and I was tired from all the travel. I felt like just sticking the gold medal on a plane and sending it around everywhere, because most of the time that was all people wanted to see.

'Did you bring the medal?' would be the first question every time.

Don't get me wrong: life as an Olympic champion was amazing. If I caught myself starting to complain about my full diary, I would just cast my mind back a few months. Problem solved.

I was certainly the subject of a lot more whispering in public.

'That's Sally Pearson,' I'd regularly hear as people did their best to pretend not to be looking my way.

For example, if I was in a line at the airport, I'd watch with amusement as they'd do a stretch and casually glance my way to confirm what their partner had told them. I'd rather they came over and said hello, but at least they knew my name now. I was no longer just the runner girl.

* * *

It was going to be fun.

I'd always wanted to find out how I'd go as a sprinter against the very best, and Sharon and I had agreed that 2013 was the year to find out. Given I'd achieved everything I wanted to do in hurdling, the new challenge of becoming a 100m sprinter again appealed to me. I wanted to see how the best sprinters did it and get a feel for the mechanics of the event. How did they go so fast?

I would still defend my hurdles crown at the world championships in Moscow later in the year, as there was a four-day gap between the 100m final and the hurdles, which was why we could experiment on the flat.

The plan involved getting the A-standard qualifying time (11.28) for the 100m during the Australian domestic season because I didn't want the hassle of chasing it in Europe. I blew the cobwebs out with a couple of easy runs at inter-club meets on the Gold Coast, but the Sydney Track Classic on 9 March was the event we'd targeted.

Everything was on track. Mentally I was ready to go again, but a training mishap that came out of the blue told a different story about my body. We were doing some starts out of blocks on the back straight when I felt something in my hamstring. The pain went away as quickly as it had come, so I figured it was a cramp. To be on the safe side, I sat out the next rep – but then it started to ache.

'It's a tear,' I declared to Sharon, who was as shocked as I was. There'd been no warning signs. I'd had no awareness at all anywhere in the leg during that session or in the weeks leading up to it.

I was totally bewildered, and my mood worsened a couple of weeks later when I attended the Sydney meet as a commentator and watched Melissa Breen benefit from ideal conditions to run a personal best 11.25 and book a place in the 100m in Moscow. While I was thrilled for her, I was spewing that I wasn't in the race.

Instead of sitting at home sulking, I took up an offer to work as an on-field commentator at the remaining events of the domestic season. The injury cleared up quickly but we were being ultra-conservative, so I was spending a lot of time in the pool.

During my lay-off I'd missed a relay run in Brisbane where the Australian team was going to attempt to get the world championships qualifying time. During the national championships in Sydney, at a planning meeting with head coach Eric Hollingsworth about the year ahead, I raised the status of the relay.

'What are we doing about this relay?' I asked. 'Are we going to try to qualify anywhere?'

He wasn't too ambitious about it because none of the other girls were running fast enough.

'We can try and get into the Asia Grand Prix series; there's one in Thailand and one in Sri Lanka,' he said.

'Let's just see how the girls run here.'

I was excited about the idea because it meant I got to leave the country early. I was always looking for ways to get overseas as quickly as possible, and when I watched Ashley Whittaker run 11.53 in the 100m final, I knew the trip was on. There was enough there to work with, and Sharon, who was the relay coach, agreed that we could definitely qualify in Thailand.

Kieran and I arrived there first and had a nice relaxing day by the pool at the Novotel Hotel at the airport. We then met the rest of the relay girls and headed to Chonburi, where the event was being held. My dreamy sunbaking mindset was quickly washed away, replaced by the loud noise of traffic – the stadium was in the middle of an industrial area.

To qualify we needed to break 44 seconds. I ran the third leg and Melissa had done the second because we didn't want the two inexperienced girls, Ashley and Monica Brennan, to have to do two changes. While I got through unscathed, unfortunately we missed the time by just .06 of a second. It meant everything was riding on Sri Lanka.

None of the team or my inner circle had been there before, so we were going into the unknown, and Mum was coming along for the adventure as she'd decided to meet us there to celebrate her 60th birthday. But it's fair to say the trip there didn't leave any of us in a celebrating mood. After arriving in Sri Lanka around 9 pm, we found out that our accommodation had been changed without anyone informing us. This wasn't just an inconvenience; it was a major problem.

Being the Olympic champion, I was one of a limited number of top-level athletes who were part of the World Anti-Doping Agency's whereabouts program. This meant drug testers needed to know where I was every day of the year. These out-of-competition tests were seen as the best way for WADA to find cheats and protect the integrity of the sport. I had a log-on to the WADA website, where I submitted my travel plans and accommodation. If I wasn't where I said I would be and testers arrived, that could be counted as a strike against my name.

If you miss three tests, you're banned – and excuses like an unexpected change in hotels isn't accepted, which was why I was anxious about the latest development. Plus Mum was getting in at 1 am and she was meeting us at the original hotel.

It took more than an hour to get from the airport to the new hotel, where we had to spend a couple of hours in the lobby while they sorted out rooms for us.

The airline food claimed its first victim with Kendra Hubbard, a member of the Australia B-team (which was also racing in the series to get some experience), sprinting out of the hotel, vomiting.

It was past midnight by the time I got into my room and I crashed straightaway.

The phone woke me in the morning; it was Mum, who'd arrived safely and figured out what had happened with all the changes. I managed a few words but that was about it – I felt like I'd been hit by a bus. I had a massive headache, my neck and shoulders were stiff, and there were sharp pains in my stomach. I wasn't the only one suffering and Sharon was forced to cancel training because there were only two girls in our travelling party who weren't sick. It turned out seven people who'd been on our flight from Bangkok, including five Singapore athletes, had been hospitalised.

But what was fast becoming the trip from hell had yet another twist to come. While we all managed to get over our stomach bugs by race day, another problem reared its ugly head again. I was running the third leg and was 30 metres away from Ashley when I tore my hamstring. I slowed down dramatically and barely got the baton to her. I don't even know what happened after that. I think we got disqualified, but I was in a daze. My world title defence was over.

Missing another slab of training would be a disaster, because history showed that playing catch-up leading into a major championship was almost impossible.

'My season is over,' were my first words to Sharon. 'I've just torn my hamstring. I have to get out of here.'

Ashley was upset because she thought it was her fault that we didn't qualify, as she had no idea about my injury. I put her mind to rest before heading to the warm-up track, where the officials kept the media away from me. I was in no mood for talking.

Getting out of Sri Lanka was all I was thinking about, but that was on hold as plans had been put in place for Mum's birthday celebration. We'd been invited to an official function by the president of Sri Lankan athletics, which was an hour-and-a-half drive from the hotel. It was good to see a bit more of the country, as we had to go through a number of small villages to get to the venue. But we only got through the entree before excusing ourselves; my brave face had a limited time span and I wanted to get out of there.

We'd decided not to go back to Australia but push on to England as planned.

'You can't go back to Australia because your motivation will just slip and you probably won't end up going back to Europe and racing at the world champs,' Mum said.

She was right. We also had a physio and massage therapist with us in England, so I would be getting the best treatment possible.

I'd never been so happy to see a cold, wet and dreary London. The first thing we did was go down to the local fish and chip shop for a hit of greasy comfort food. It was a one-off, but so badly needed given the horrors of the past couple of weeks.

The next 48 hours were a rollercoaster. My first diagnosis was horrifying: I'd had an ultrasound and the doctor claimed it showed a 5-centimetre tear in the hamstring. We got a second opinion the following day, with an MRI scan that thankfully showed there was actually only a 1-centimetre tear in the hamstring. That totally changed our mindset and dramatically reduced the rehab time, which was the lucky break I needed.

But I was still grumpy. Very grumpy. It's hard to be told that all you can do is be patient. That was something I'd never been good at and it was times like those when Sharon showed her strength by putting up with me.

Slowly the hamstring started to improve over the next couple of weeks, and to keep my head clear, Kieran and I played tourists. While I'd done all the tourist things many times before, I still got a kick out of getting out and looking at London at its finest. We ticked off Buckingham Palace, Covent Garden, the London Eye and Windsor Castle and had a night at the theatre seeing *Les Miserables*.

Everything was progressing until I had a meltdown at training. My senses were clearly heightened when it came to my hamstring, and I was convinced I'd torn it again when I pulled up sharply during a run-through. It was exactly the same feeling I'd had in Sri Lanka, so I freaked out. The medical staff didn't think I'd torn it, and we agreed to give it a couple of days off and then test it again.

I was angry because we'd just locked in my return at the Oslo Diamond League, but that wasn't going to happen now because my body had failed me again. I tried to train but the hamstring was tight.

Sharon had been away in Edinburgh with a couple of my training partners so had missed the initial incident, but she could tell something wasn't right. The problem was I'd had so much treatment, so much rehab, that I was just over it. My spirit had been drained.

'Just go away for a couple of days,' Sharon said. 'Leave treatment, leave training, just go.'

As soon as she said that I felt an instant weight off my shoulders.

'I'm going tonight,' I declared.

For everyone's sake, I had to clear my mind. It was out of character for me to take a break from training, but that showed how down I was. Once the decision was made, I was instantly a different person and had a beaming smile on my face as Kieran and I walked into the travel agency.

'We want to go somewhere hot, and we want to leave tonight,' I said.

My ignorance of Europe became evident, as I thought we could just jump on a plane, click our fingers and we'd be on a nice sunny beach. That wasn't the case, but the compromise was a good one: Paris. The 'somewhere hot' thinking was replaced with 'somewhere where I can eat a lot of amazing food', which was why the French capital had jumped to the top of the list, and I was very excited as I typed our accommodation details into my WADA whereabouts profile. It was an inspired choice, and for three days we let our hair down and indulged.

I'm an emotional eater. I eat when I'm happy, sad and stressed. The latter two had certainly been the case over the past month. I kept a record of our dining for the blog I was starting on my new website, which was a business venture Kieran and I had been working on for some time. It was an impressive list that included caramel and chocolate slice, cheeseburgers and fries, croissants, lemon pie, calamari, macaroni and cheese, lemon tart, doughnuts, crepes, and ham and pineapple pizza. That was only a rough draft, too – there could have been more. It was outrageous on so many levels, but not once did I think about my hamstring during it – which was the aim of the whole trip.

By the end of the third day I felt disgusting and was looking forward to exercising again. When I returned to training I was a different person. The key to optimal performance in training and competition is motivation, and now it was back – and, according to Sharon, so was my speed over the hurdles. She even compared it to what I had been demonstrating in the lead-up to the Olympics.

As a consequence we decided to add more races to my schedule and now had six planned in the lead-up to the world championships, kicking off on 27 June at the Ostrava Golden Spike World Challenge in the Czech Republic.

Just a few days before my kick-off, the landscape in the 100m hurdles changed significantly: there was a new kid on the block in a big way. At the US trials, college champion Brianna Rollins ran faster than I had in Daegu, clocking 12.26 to become the third fastest in history. Initially I was a bit shocked, then pissed off, then motivated. I didn't like anyone being faster than me, so I had some work to do.

Getting back on the circuit felt strange, and when we got to Ostrava I realised I'd forgotten about the most annoying aspect of race day: the waiting. I spent all day trying to fill in time. There were a few Skype sessions to family back home and then I watched the movie *Despicable Me* before finally heading out to the track, where, as usual, I was early.

It was good to be back in the atmosphere of a track meet, and I soaked it up while I warmed up. I was first into the call room for the heat, and as I sat there waiting, the nerves hit. This got me excited because I hadn't had that feeling for so long. Once I got there and did a couple of practice runs, I felt settled and ready.

That certainly wasn't how I was feeling, though, when I annihilated the sixth hurdle and almost stopped. I managed to pick myself up and get going again to cross the line in 12.90! I couldn't even remember the last time I ran 12.90. It had been disgusting, and the hurdling almost felt foreign to my body.

'Let's go a bit faster in the final, shall we?' I said to Sharon.

The heat run had at least blown the cobwebs out, and there were a few given it had been ten months since I'd run a hurdles race, and I certainly felt a lot more comfortable lining up for the final. Everything felt a lot more normal as I got my trademark fast start, and at the seventh hurdle I almost lost concentration because I was so excited that I hadn't hit a hurdle.

I kept it going and crossed the line in 12.67.

'Yeeeessssss!' My little squeal of delight showed the relief I felt. That was the fastest time I'd ever run in my first hurdles race of any campaign. There had been no issues with the hamstring, and my agent summed it up best: 'I could see the rust coming off you with each hurdle.'

Next was my return to the big time at the Diamond League meet in Birmingham three days later. It was good to be back in the company of Dawn Harper and Kellie Wells, the placegetters from the London Olympics. I was certainly going to find out exactly where I was in the scheme of things after this race.

With two hurdles to go, I got the answer. After matching the girls over the first half of the race, my lack of fitness told over the final couple of hurdles and I faded to finish fourth in 12.74. Harper had won in 12.64 from Wells (12.67) with Tiffany Porter (12.73) just getting me for third.

More than anyone on the planet, I hated getting beaten. But I understood the reasons for that defeat, which helped ease the pain. I'd missed a lot of work and a lot of racing while those girls hadn't. They had an advantage at the moment, but at least I was finally starting to make up ground.

There was again only a short break between races, but it was unavoidable because I was playing catch-up. The Lausanne Diamond League was one of my favourites because Switzerland was such a beautiful place and I could spend hours just sitting there staring out at the stunning mountains. I'd also found a secret little chocolate shop, which I visited every year. This chocolate was incredible, mouth-watering goodness, and the perfect treat after my race, of course.

Unfortunately I didn't have anything to celebrate. In my worst result for years, I again faded late in the race and finished seventh in 12.69. I was stunned more than anything, and in a confused daze as I made my way back to the warm-up track.

Harper had won again in 12.53, and the next six athletes were split by less than .2 of a second. It had been the same story. I'd started well and was with the rest of the girls at halfway, but the tail end of my race had been poor.

'Aren't I supposed to be getting better, not worse?' was the question I posed to Sharon.

I certainly wasn't in the mood to be making appearances at VIP functions, but a brave face was put on at the official afterparty. In the end I'm glad I went because I bumped into Olympic 400m champion Felix Sanchez and his agent, TC. They knew I wasn't happy and went out of their way to cheer me up.

Felix had won Olympic gold in Athens in 2004 and then came back eight years later and did it again in London, so he knew a bit about the ups and downs of the sport.

'As a champion you have to lose to learn to appreciate the wins,' he said. 'Never accept defeat but learn from it and it will make you stronger in the end.'

I didn't know how to take that at the time, but later I understood where he was coming from. I was definitely not accepting what was happening and was learning how to deal with it in the best way. I wasn't going to shy away from the competition; I would keep turning up and trying my hardest to be the athlete I had been over the previous two years.

No-one said it was going to be easy, and there was still six weeks until the world championships and a lot of hurdles to get over before then. The search for answers took us off the beaten track to a low-key event in Sotteville, France. This seemed to have 'confidence boost' written all over it, given the line-up, but it was the complete opposite.

I walked off that track a gutted athlete. The same thing had happened again: I was vying for the lead until the final two hurdles, and then there was nothing. Two Americans who hadn't even made the world championships team had beaten me. I struggled into third in 12.76.

I was the Olympic champion, and yet I felt like I couldn't get out of my own way. My training had been improving but I wasn't getting the results out on the track. For the first time I really started to wonder where I was at.

There was an 11-day gap until my next race in Monaco and the only thing we could do was hit the training track and keep working. As hard as that was, given all the anxiety buzzing around in my mind, it was, a tried and true formula and we had to stick to it.

I wasn't a good person to be around during that time.

By Sharon's calculation I had cleared 150 fewer hurdles in training that year than I usually had before I started racing. That said a lot, which was why my coach was cramming in some intensive hurdle workouts to search for the missing link.

My good history in Monaco at least gave me something to go with – plus new American sensation Brianna Rollins was expected to be there. I was intrigued to finally get a look at her, but when we arrived in town we found out she was a no-show. There was a rumour that her management didn't want her to race me before Moscow, and I was asked my thoughts about the 21-year-old American at the event press conference.

The other line of questioning was disturbing, given it centred around the shocking news of the positive drug tests by two of the fastest men in the world, American Tyson Gay and Jamaica's former world record holder Asafa Powell. I was particularly saddened about Asafa, as I'd had a bit to do with him when he had come out and raced in Australia in recent years. It was a major blow to the sport and I was bemused that supplements were being blamed for the positive tests.

Some athletes took dozens of the little capsules – I took none. I knew I got everything I needed by eating properly, with meat, fruit and vegetables providing the same thing as those dodgy supplements. Other athletes always looked shocked when I suggested they eat more food rather than take more pills.

These supplement companies were making a mint for capsules that didn't always contain what the label said was supposed to be in them. The result was that more and more athletes were being disqualified and run out of the sport. I just didn't understand – why take the risk?

I certainly wasn't thinking about the drugs controversy as I lined up inside the stadium that had been so good to me in the past. The key words being 'in the past' – because it wasn't this time. As soon as I crossed the line in fifth – I clocked 12.75, with American Queen Harrison winning in 12.64 – the first words that entered my mind were: 'I can't be bothered anymore.' It felt like we'd tried every trick in the book and nothing was changing. I was still getting run over late in my races by girls who normally wouldn't be anywhere near me.

The gala dinner in Monaco after the meet was normally a highlight, but not that year. We were again seated at the prince's table, but just before the dinner was about to commence Aries Merritt came over. The American was my male contemporary, as he had won the gold medal in the 110m hurdles at the London Olympics and was also the world record holder.

'I'm going to take her away for a little bit and have a chat with her,' he told Kieran and Sharon.

'Okay,' I said warily, as I had no idea what he wanted.

As we sat down he said: 'Don't be down on yourself, don't be down – these girls are scared of you.'

'Are you serious?' I said. 'Have they not seen my times?'

'Yes, they have – but they know who you are,' Aries said. 'They know what you have done and you know what you have done. You can do it; you can come back from it.' Aries had also suffered hamstring injuries earlier in the season but had fought back and had recently won at the Paris Grand Prix.

'I bet you've only done one speed session,' he said.

Damn. How did he know that? I wanted to be right about everything and just continue to sulk, but Aries wouldn't have it.

'I was rooting for you as I know what you're going through,' he said. 'I've been in the same position and I'm still in the same position. I'm still not at my best.'

I disagreed on that point. 'You won in Paris so you're not in the same position as me,' I said. 'You've also done your hamstring a couple of times this year but I'm coming last in my races, almost.'

He was trying to cheer me up and it was working because it was nice to know people like him cared.

'Don't you be down,' he continued. 'You have to start right now thinking you are going to win the world championships because if you're not thinking that then you have lost it.

'You have to start now. Start thinking you're going to win the world championships.'

He then paused and moved in closer to me.

'I believe in you.'

When you're at the track, every light bulb has to be on and ready for what you're about to do.

19

It was times like those when I appreciated the 'Sharon Factor'.

To me, a coach is the most important part of my training, my confidence, my talent and of course my preparation. There is no way I would be as good as I am today without my dedicated coach. She is on a mission to become the best athletics coach she can be, whether that's coaching me or coaching club-level athletes.

Sharon just loves to coach, and you can hear in her voice how passionate she is about the sport and about learning how to better herself so she can help athletes achieve their goals. To me that is a very selfless act, especially considering athletes can be very selfish people who only care about being the best athlete they can be – me included.

I don't say thank you enough to the people who have my best interests at heart, and who have helped me to become the best athlete in the world. My mission, as well as being the best athlete I can be, is to be more aware of the people around me and to make sure they know how appreciative I am of their efforts.

Sharon had been by my side for 14 years and, more than ever, I needed her magic to work. As usual she had a theory about what had been going wrong. She'd analysed all my races and had figured out that my hurdle clearances over the whole race were only .12 slower than Daegu. But the speed in between the hurdles over the whole race was .4 slower, which is almost half a second. What was stopping me from running fast was the speed in between the hurdles. It was great to have some kind of explanation of what was going on.

We both knew there was enough time to get that speed back before Moscow, but could I get it back in time for my final lead-up race in London? There was something extra-special about the event because it was being held in the Olympic Stadium. The thought of going back to where all my dreams had come true 12 months earlier was the shot of excitement I needed.

Add that to the fact that I could feel things starting to click after some solid speed sessions at training and I felt a bit like the old me again. There was certainly a familiarity about the warm-up, and it actually felt like the Olympics.

When I entered the stadium, the memories came flooding back, as once again, there was not a spare seat in the house. It was an incredible atmosphere, and it went up a level when Jessica Ennis, the heptathlon gold medalist who was in my 100m hurdles event, was introduced.

As I got on the blocks I figured that surely these circumstances would bring something special out. At halfway I smiled and said to myself: 'Oh, thank God.'

It was nice finally to feel like I knew how to hurdle again. I felt smooth and was already well clear of the other girls. I was cautious over the final two hurdles because I didn't want any mistakes; I just wanted to get to the finish line first.

When I achieved that, I looked at the clock, which read 12.65. I was hoping for faster but, importantly, I knew there was a lot more in me.

You couldn't wipe the smile from my face afterwards, and it turned out I'd won comfortably from Britain's Tiffany Porter (12.76) and American Kellie Wells (12.95). I was actually more relieved than I'd been at the Olympics because it had been such a tough month.

For the first time in a while, I was happy to front the press and decided to deliver a message to those who'd written me off.

'It's hard when you are Olympic and world champion and getting absolutely smashed in races and having bad comments about you,' I said. '[But] it's nice today to come out and know that I am a champion and I know how to get the job done.'

Two days later I was on the massage table with my good friend Bruno in Tonbridge and, as usual, he was relaying his theories on life. One of them I liked a lot.

'The difference is you're just running with them now,' Bruno said.

'They're running the same as they always do this time of the year but you're running with them. They are used to you being out in front. The thing is: because you're running with them, they think they can beat you now, which is hilarious because they can't. You're getting better and better and they're just staying the same as they always do.'

Bruno was on the money again. I was getting better.

* * *

It was so fast.

Given how I'd felt so slow for the past few months, the quickness of the warm-up track in Moscow was unnerving.

My first session had been a disaster. If a track is fast, it can throw out your rhythm, as your body and mind aren't working in tandem with the spring and bounce you're getting off the ground. This all adds up to one big mess for a hurdler.

I was becoming more and more frustrated as my second hurdling session started the same way. I was getting too close to the hurdles, and it almost felt like I didn't know what I was doing.

'Why can't I hurdle? I kept asking Sharon. 'What if this happens on the real track at the stadium?'

It was freaking me out because I'd worked so hard to get my speed back and to feel normal again; then I'd arrived at the world championships and all the good work seemed to have gone out the window.

Patience. Patience. Patience.

I was sick of hearing the word from my coach, but she was sticking by it. The key was we had plenty of time, as we'd arrived in Moscow on the Tuesday before the championships commenced on the Saturday. Well, they commenced for a lot of people then – my first-round heat wasn't until the following Friday.

I found the waiting around particularly tough. While the program had been exactly the same in Daegu, I seemed to forget how long the wait felt every time. Staying focused on the job can be quite tough when you're scheduled at the end of the program.

You have to remain calm and relaxed, but at the same time remember that you have a job to do and remind your body that it's not time to shut down yet. It's a delicate balancing act, because if you're thinking about things all the time, then your body stays tense, which is not ideal.

The key is to know when it's okay to switch off and switch on. This takes years of trial and error to get right. Ideally when you're not at the track, then you switch your mind and body off – but when you're at the track, every light bulb has to be on and ready for what you're about to do.

As a young athlete there are always people giving you advice on how to do this, but it comes down to experience. There will be some disappointing moments as you learn how to deal with these situations, but it's how you deal with them the next time and the one after that which will make you a better athlete.

I found I was best suited to sticking to the same routine. The 4x100m boys, who were also at the end of the program and dealing with the same issues, refer to it as 'Groundhog Day' – which just happens to be one of my favourite movies.

With my heat scheduled for 9.30 am on the Friday, I trained myself to wake early, like I would on race morning, when I'd be required to catch the 7 am bus to the warm-up track to start preparation.

This meant that for the four days leading up, I had the alarm set for 6 am. I would get up, go downstairs for breakfast to kill a bit of time, and then head back up to the room to watch the morning session or another episode of the popular TV series *Suits*, which had been recommended to me by Bruno. He'd warned me that it was addictive and had suggested to everyone on the team to get involved. Good old Bruno was right again – I was hooked.

At lunchtime I'd wander down to the foyer of the Crowne Plaza Hotel, where were staying, and have a chat to whoever was about. Staying in a hotel is very different from the vibe and atmosphere of an athletes' village. I prefer the village style, because there you share an apartment complex with six or eight girls and there's a communal area where you can all sit and chat. There was nothing like that in Moscow.

My roommate was javelin thrower Kathryn Mitchell, who was also competing at the back end of the program, but she had her own routine and we really didn't see much of each other.

There were a number of other teams, including the US, who were staying in the same hotel, so the foyer was a hive of activity and I'd regularly bump into a couple of my rivals.

Kieran, Mum and my manager, Robert, were all staying at a different hotel, so I'd often kill a part of the afternoon by meeting them and going for a walk up to one of the shopping centres that were about a kilometre from the hotel.

In the lead-up to the start of the championships, I'd had the opportunity to see a few of the sights of Moscow while I did some media events. The IAAF press call was in the famous Red Square, and I was pleased to get a few snaps there with some of my counterparts, including the lovely Allyson Felix, the 200m Olympic champion.

I'd picked up another title to put alongside my name for these championships, which was a great honour. Now I had Australian Flame captain to go with Olympic champion and defending world champion.

I had some big shoes to fill, as Steve Hooker had been sensational in the role, but he wasn't in Moscow so the baton had been passed to me. I actually took a little time to think about it before accepting, but then I realised there was a generational change happening that would make it easier.

What excited me was the fact that there were so many new faces in the Australian team – 19 debutants to be exact – and I figured I could make a big difference in helping them to understand what it's like to be an international athlete at a world championships. Sometimes it can be quite overwhelming, and while I obviously had to make sure the role didn't take away from my own preparation, I was confident I could help my teammates. I also had an able deputy in javelin thrower Kim Mickle, who was the life of the team and a seriously funny girl.

I found myself being chief cheerleader a couple of times.

Each evening I would be locked into watching the athletics. The performance of Flame teammate Zoe Buckman as she won her 1500m heat, and then the semifinal, had me jumping around on my bed.

The night before my heat I was down in the foyer watching the action with Sharon and Kathryn and was literally out of my seat cheering when Tristan Thomas ran an amazing final leg in the heats of the 4x400m relay to get the Australian team through to the final. He'd received the baton in fifth position but surged over the top in the final 150 metres to grab second.

It was inspiring stuff but I figured I needed to calm it down a touch, as I needed a good night's sleep. My day had finally arrived.

It wasn't in my nature to go down without a fight. I'd fought all year just to make it ... so I was going to focus on doing the best I could ...

20

The panic was gone but the nerves had arrived, big time.

While I'd struggled in my opening couple of training sessions in Moscow, my final two had been on the money and I felt I was finally in control of my hurdling again.

The waiting around clearly contributed to my nerves. The recent victory in London seemed like months ago rather than a few weeks, and I just wanted to get the heat underway, stay upright and get to finals day as quickly as possible.

My start was on the money, which was a relief in itself, and I felt good as I moved through the race before something went amiss at the ninth hurdle. I'm not sure if I lost concentration but I made a mess of it and then I was awfully crooked coming over the last hurdle.

I was never in any danger of falling or getting beaten, but it was going to hurt my time. There was a hint of frustration as I looked over at the clock as I crossed the line to see 12.62. While it was my fastest time for the year, it wasn't exactly the shot of confidence I was after. And my intention to follow the Daegu and London script of being the fastest through all the rounds was already out the window, as Rollins had won her heat in 12.55.

The positive was that I was feeling sparky again. There were times during the race where I felt fast and I knew I would be able to be cleaner and eradicate the mistakes at the end of the semifinal. I was pleased to see I was in the third semifinal the following night, which gave me the opportunity to watch my rivals and see their times before I ran.

What didn't please me was the line-up. It was stacked, and I couldn't believe they were making the defending champion work that hard. I had Dawn Harper on one side and another American, Queen Harrison, on the other. Great Britain's Tiffany Porter had no-one of note in the opening semi, while Rollins also had a much easier assignment in the second.

The first two placegetters in each semi were automatically through to the final, plus the next two fastest.

I'd watched Dawn in the heats and, surprisingly, she'd struggled, finishing third in 12.84. I wondered what had gone wrong with her, but she was a competitor and would be bringing something more in the semifinal.

'I'm going to have to be on my game,' I said to Sharon.

As expected, Porter was untroubled, winning the first semi in 12.63, and I was pleasantly surprised when Rollins only ran 12.54 to get victory in the next.

This was where the benefit of being the last run came to the fore. I knew exactly what I needed to produce to be the fastest qualifier and send a message to a few people.

As we mingled behind the blocks, I knew I was going to have to push hard, but for the first time for the year I felt I could.

I was right.

I flew the start like the old me and was clearly ahead over the first. I could sense Dawn had gone with me until just over halfway, but there weren't going to be any mistakes this time and I nailed the final two hurdles.

As I hit the line there was no Dawn, and the clock read 12.50.

'Yeessss,' I said, and I even slipped in a small fist pump as I crossed the line. The race had been brilliant. I'd run the fastest time and made a statement in the process: Don't write me off.

I may have had a horrible year, but this was what I could still do. It was like I was saying, 'Don't get comfortable, girls, because I'm going to be fighting every inch of that final.'

People can be very quick to judge an athlete, but I'd never written off a champion before in a race – because they'd been there and done it.

I'd been there and done it too. I'd just brought the experience and determination that I'd used in every single championships to my race, and it had clearly paid off.

By the time I'd got downstairs, met Sharon and got onto the bus to take us to the warm-up track, there were only 21 minutes until we were due back in the call room for the final. There was usually so much more time. Maybe it was because I'd been in the last semifinal that it felt shorter, but we were both thrown out a bit, even though I generally don't do much in between the two races.

While I was excited about the semifinal, there was one troubling aspect. I'd worked hard to run 12.50, and I could feel it. There were so many questions going through my mind. Could I repeat it? Could I go faster? I hadn't run anything near that all year, so how was I going to back it up inside 90 minutes? Did Rollins have more to give?

My legs had that wonderful tingly feeling that you only experience after a particularly fast race. But which tingly feeling was it? The 'ready to go again' tingle or the 'absolutely fatigued' tingle? All this was going on in my head as I lay on the massage table and tried to get my breathing back to normal after the exertion of the semifinal.

In the back of my mind I'd carried around the nagging feeling that I wasn't going to win gold in Moscow. It had been with me for a while, obviously born out of all the setbacks I'd experienced throughout the campaign.

After initially thinking my world championships were over when I tore my hamstring for the second time, once I'd started back and slowly regained fitness, I had said that my expectation was to medal in Moscow. I'd never stated what colour it was going to be. And now, just minutes away from heading out onto the track, I sensed it wasn't going to be gold.

It was almost like I felt I didn't deserve it because I hadn't done all the work that I knew you needed to do to become a world champion.

Before the Daegu final, after I'd run the fastest time of my life in the semifinal, I'd asked Sharon if I'd run my legs out. That time I knew the answer was no and I was just seeking reassurance.

This time I wasn't so sure.

'No, you haven't,' my coach said in her wonderfully positive manner.

I really couldn't be disappointed with anything from that point on. I knew I should be proud that I was on the start line for the world championships final. But it wasn't in my nature to go down without a fight. I'd fought all year just to make it, and funny things can happen in sport, so I was going to focus on doing the best I could and see if a miracle happened.

Standing behind the blocks, I was feeling positive and tall, and that told me I was going to run well; if I'm standing tall and have my shoulders back and head up, the hurdles look really small. That was how I'd felt before the start of the semifinal, as well. I felt tall and strong.

As I'd struggled through Europe that year, my shoulders had been down behind the blocks. When I looked down the track at the hurdles they'd felt like they were 10 feet tall and I'd be asking myself: 'What the hell am I doing here?' But I knew what I was doing this time. I was drawn in lane six, with Harper in five and Porter in four. Rollins was on my outside in lane seven.

Okay. This is it. You can do this.

The starter seemed to hold us for a long time, and the crowd, which had quietened, briefly came to life again before I finally heard the gun. I got away clean and fast and was in front over the first hurdle.

You're leading. You're leading. Go. Go.

I was in exactly the same place as I'd been in the previous two races. At halfway I was in front, but there was a different thought process.

Where are you? Where are you?

In the semifinal I'd been telling myself I had the race; this time I was waiting for Rollins. I knew she had a good end to her races, and at the sixth hurdle I felt her presence.

Go now. Faster. Faster.

I surged over the seventh.

I've got her. Miracles do happen … Wait!

At the eighth hurdle Rollins came again and had serious momentum.

I've lost it. I knew it. There's not going to be a gold.

I couldn't go any faster. I'd managed a little burst, but she had more.

What the hell? Who's that on my inside?

I'd noticed earlier that Porter had got a good start, and with two hurdles to get over she was almost in front of me.

Holy crap. No way you're going past me as well!

I was hurting but scraped everything I had left to keep my nose in front and held it to the line.

Silver! I deserved that.

While there was instant disappointment about not winning, because that was built into who I was, it was quickly replaced by relief and a sense of pride. There had been so many times when I'd thought about pulling the pin and not coming to Moscow, but I'd persevered and I had a silver medal to show for it.

Rollins had run 12.44 to win, while I'd replicated my semifinal run of 12.50. Porter got the bronze in 12.55, with Harper fourth in 12.59.

'How good is it to have that race over?' I said to Porter as we congratulated each other.

'Ohhhh, it's so good,' she said.

It had been a long season for everyone. While I was glad it was over, the final had been a great race. It had been close and I'd really enjoyed it, although I never thought 12.50 was going to feel that hard to do.

The victory lap felt a bit different but I still loved having the Australian flag draped over my shoulders. It also gave me an opportunity to digest the race, and I soon realised that while I didn't have the gold, I was going to come away from Moscow the real winner.

Those girls should have smashed in that race. They had everything in their favour, yet I'd only been beaten by one of them by just .06 of a second. In those conditions Rollins should have been able to run 12.2, and Porter should have beaten me and improved her personal best by a lot more than 1/100th of a second.

It showed me that on the day I'd been the better athlete.

Going forward I was going to be full of confidence because next time I wouldn't be chasing my tail in the lead-up – Sharon calculated I'd missed a great many hurdle clearances in training because of the injuries – and I would still be the best hurdler.

The only thing was I didn't have the title to show for it this time. As I made my way through the mixed zone, I darted off halfway through to see Sharon. I knew how much stress she'd been under and all I wanted to do was give her a big hug.

She had a present for me from my physio, Kerrie – a packet of Tim Tams attached to a piece of string, which Sharon then presented to me like a medal and placed around my neck. I'd asked Kerrie to bring them over from Australia because it was the chocolate hit I'd been craving and I was planning on rewarding myself with them after the championships had ended.

There were more media interviews to be done, but the medal ceremony wasn't until the following evening so there was no rush.

'It is a satisfying medal placing,' I told the assembled print journalists:

'It's been very hard for me this year and I think I owe everything that I have done to Sharon tonight. We have both been on a very big emotional rollercoaster, and I almost didn't make it to these championships through all the emotional time that I have had.

'I don't think I could probably ask for anything more. I pushed that race as hard as I could and, as I have been saying and Sharon has been saying, I've missed probably 150 hurdle clearances and you can definitely tell out there that I have missed those sessions.

'I'm very proud at how I handled myself at these championships. I ran through each round with a season best and I wasn't expecting that.

'We have to remember that a champion knows how to do it on the night and I was able to do that. I don't think I can ask for anything more but silver is not going to happen again.'

The champagne flowed that night as my team celebrated in the foyer of the hotel. Sharon was going home in a couple of days, but I was going to race on for another month throughout Europe because it was silly to pull the pin now that I'd finally gotten myself back into shape.

I was already looking ahead to defending my world indoor title next year, and the Glasgow Commonwealth Games were going to be a lot more interesting than before, given Porter's improvement and the fact that Canada's Angela Whyte, another Commonwealth athlete, had finished sixth in the final.

Once there, I would again draw on the three words that had been the cornerstone of my performance in Moscow and throughout my whole career.

Focus. Determination. Believe.

Some people might look at them as just words, but I say them over and over and over again. All the time. They are the most important principles to stand by for the hurdles, and it takes time to learn how to turn the words into actions.

I've learnt so much from the ups and downs I've gone through as I've figured out the sport, figured out where I belonged in the sport and then, importantly, learnt that I did belong.

There were so many times when my opponents might have been faster than me, but I came to realise that didn't mean I shouldn't be in that race as well. The key is to never be overwhelmed by an opponent or an occasion.

A lot has to do with your personality type. People get nervous when they race and that's why they falter. But for me, the more nervous I get, the better I do. I've learnt to deal with the occasion by telling myself that nerves are okay. It's a sign that I'm ready, that I care about what I'm going to do and that I'm passionate about the race I'm about to run.

I find that if I stay focused on the specifics of what I have to do at the start and during the race when I'm nervous, then I'm able to deal with it.

But most of all, above anything else, I *believe*.

Achievements

2011 Awarded Female Athlete of the Year by the IAAF
2011 World Champion in 100m hurdles
2012 Olympic Champion in 100m hurdles

MEDAL RECORD

Olympics
Gold	2012	London	100m hurdles
Silver	2008	Beijing	100m hurdles

World Championships
Gold	2011	Daegu	100m hurdles
Silver	2013	Moscow	100m hurdles

World Indoor Athletics Championships
Gold	2012	Istanbul	60m hurdles

Commonwealth Games
Gold	2010	Delhi	100m hurdles
Bronze	2006	Melbourne	4x100m relay

Continental Cup
Gold	2010	Split	100m hurdles

World Junior Championships
Bronze   2004   Grosseto   100m

World Youth Championships
Gold   2003   Sherbrooke   100m hurdles

Major International Competitions

2003	1st	100m hurdles	World Youth Championships	Sherbrooke, Canada
2003	5th	200m	World Youth Championships	Sherbrooke, Canada
2004	4th	100m hurdles	World Junior Championships	Paris, France
2004	3rd	100m	World Junior Championships	Paris, France
2004	5th	4x100m	World Junior Championships	Paris, France
2006	8th	100m	Commonwealth Games	Melbourne, Australia
2006	4th	100m hurdles	World Cup	Athens, Greece
2006	8th	100m	World Cup	Athens, Greece
2007	Semi-finals	100m	World Championships	Osaka, Japan
2007	Semi-finals	100m hurdles	World Championships	Osaka, Japan
2008	2nd	100m hurdles	Olympic Games	Beijing, China
2009	5th	100m hurdles	World Championships	Berlin, Germany
2010	1st	100m hurdles	Commonwealth Games	New Delhi, India
2011	1st	100m hurdles	World Championships	Daegu, South Korea
2012	1st	60m hurdles	World Indoor Championships	Istanbul, Turkey
2012	1st	100m hurdles	Olympic games	London, United Kingdom
2013	2nd	100m hurdles	World Championships	Moscow, Russia

Personal Bests

	PERFORMANCE	WIND	PLACE	DATE
100m	11.14	+1.7	Osaka	26 August 2007
150m	16.86	—		1 January 2010
200m	23.02	-0.4	Gold Coast	14 June 2009
200m	23.02	+1.0	Melbourne	03 March 2012
300m	38.34	—	Gold Coast	19 December 2009
100m hurdles	12.28	+1.1	Daegu	03 September 2011
100m hurdles (76.2cm)	13.14	+0.5	Sherbrooke	11 July 2003
400m hurdles	1:02.98		Brisbane	10 November 2007
60m	7.30	—	Boston (Roxbury), MA	07 February 2009
60m hurdles	7.73	—	Istanbul	10 March 2012

Progression – outdoor

	PERFORMANCE	WIND	PLACE	DATE
100m				
2012	11.20	-1.2	Nivelles	23 June
2011	11.20	+0.5	Perth	31 March
2010	11.28	+0.2	New Delhi	07 October
2010	11.28	+1.0	New Delhi	07 October
2009	11.26	+1.9	Brisbane	22 February
2008	11.41	-0.2	Canberra	26 January
2007	11.14	+1.7	Osaka	26 August
2006	11.36	+1.4	Melbourne	20 March
2005	11.41	+1.1	Brisbane	26 November
2004	11.40	+1.5	Grosseto	14 July
2003	11.57	+1.7	Runaway Bay	12 April
150m				
2010	16.86	—	—	01 January
2006	17.94	-1.3	Geelong	02 December

	PERFORMANCE	WIND	PLACE	DATE
200m				
2012	23.02	+1.0	Melbourne	03 March
2011	23.05	+0.4	Brisbane	11 February
2010	23.19	+1.3	Sydney	27 February
2009	23.02	-0.4	Gold Coast	14 June
2008	23.55	+2.0	Gold Coast	15 June
2007	23.55	-1.4	Brisbane	22 July
2006	23.36	+0.6	Canberra	26 January
2005	23.45	-0.6	Brisbane	26 November
2004	23.90	+0.7	Runaway Bay	21 May
2003	23.78	+1.6	Brisbane	13 December
300m				
2009	38.34		Gold Coast	19 December
2006	38.65		Geelong	02 December
100m Hurdles				
2013	12.50	-0.7	Moskva (Luzhniki)	17 August
2013	12.50	-0.6	Moskva (Luzhniki)	17 August
2012	12.35	-0.2	London (OP)	07 August
2011	12.28	+1.1	Daegu	03 September
2010	12.57	+0.2	Stockholm	06 August
2009	12.50	+0.7	Monaco	28 July
2008	12.53	+0.1	Monaco	29 July
2007	12.71	0.0	Osaka	05 May
2006	12.95	-0.6	Athína (Olympic Stadium)	17 September
2005	13.01	+0.4	Brisbane	26 November
2004	13.30	+1.0	Grosseto	15 July
2003	14.01	-1.7	Sydney	22 March
100m Hurdles (76.2CM)				
2003	13.14	+0.5	Sherbrooke	11 July
400m Hurdles				
2007	1:02.98		Brisbane	10 November

Progression – indoor

	PERFORMANCE	PLACE	DATE
60m			
2009	7.30	Boston (Roxbury), MA	07 February
60m Hurdles			
2012	7.73	Istanbul	10 March
2009	7.96	New York (MSG), NY	30 January

	RANK	MARK	WIND	PLACE	DATE
100m					
11th IAAF World Championships in Athletics	8sf1	11.32	-0.3	Osaka	27 August 2007
10th IAAF World Cup	8	11.44	+0.1	Athína (Olympic Stadium)	16 September 2006
10th IAAF World Junior Championships	3	11.40	+1.5	Grosseto	14 July 2004
200m					
3rd IAAF World Youth Championships	5	24.01	-0.4	Sherbrooke	12 July 2003
60m Hurdles					
IAAF World Indoor Championships 2012	1	7.73		Istanbul	10 March 2012
100m Hurdles					
14th IAAF World Championships	2	12.50	-0.6	Moskva (Luzhniki)	17 August 2013
The XXX Olympic Games	1	12.35	-0.2	London (OP)	07 August 2012

	RANK	MARK	WIND	PLACE	DATE
13th IAAF World Championships in Athletics	1	12.28	+1.1	Daegu	03 September 2011
IAAF/VTB Bank Continental Cup 2010	1	12.65	-0.5	Split	05 September 2010
12th IAAF World Championships in Athletics	5	12.70	+0.2	Berlin	19 August 2009
6th IAAF/VTB Bank World Athletics Final	6	12.82	+0.3	Stuttgart	13 September 2008
The XXIX Olympic Games	2	12.64	+0.1	Beijing (National Stadium)	19 August 2008
11th IAAF World Championships in Athletics	5sf2	12.82	-0.1	Osaka	28 August 2007
10th IAAF World Cup	4	12.95	-0.6	Athína (Olympic Stadium)	17 September 2006
10th IAAF World Junior Championships	4	13.41	-1.0	Grosseto	16 July 2004
100m Hurdles (76.2CM)					
3rd IAAF World Youth Championships	1	13.42	-1.9	Sherbrooke	12 July 2003